POETS AND POETRY

BEING ARTICLES REPRINTED FROM THE
LITERARY SUPPLEMENT OF
'THE TIMES'

BY

JOHN BAILEY

Essay Index Reprint Series

BOOKS FOR LIBRARIES PRESS, INC.
FREEPORT, NEW YORK

First published 1911
Reprinted 1967

LIBRARY OF CONGRESS CATALOG CARD NUMBER:
67-30196

PRINTED IN THE UNITED STATES OF AMERICA

PREFACE

THE poet Rogers is reported to have had a saying, 'When a new book comes out I read an old one.' If mottoes were any longer in fashion, that remark would do as well as any I could find to put before this little volume. Not that, of course, the essays here collected carry the doctrine of ' the old is better' at all so far as Rogers. Indeed they could not well suggest the ignoring of new books; for it is to new books that they owe their existence. A man who never reads a new author is in danger of making his mind a mere museum of fossils. Or, if that puts it too strongly—for the immortals are after all the immortals, and live exempt from fears of fossil decay—yet the new are necessary interpreters of those among the old who possess genius. For it is the privilege of genius to be inexhaustible. Every generation reads Dante afresh, and for each in turn he is, or may be, new-born. If a man could exclude from his mind all subsequent literature and read Homer or Virgil just as the Alexandrian or Augustan scholars read them, he would simply have sacrificed life to archaeology, and his Homer, still more his Virgil, would be but a small fraction of the full stature of the poet, which it has taken many generations of the human mind and many races of men to see in such completeness as we can see it to-day.

The new then are necessary to the old. But even less than the old can they stand alone. That is true even of original and creative work, which builds on the sands if it forgets that the human mind is a thing of continuous life, for which all new departures must find their root and starting-point in something already accepted. Still more,

of course, is it true of such books as those which give
occasion to the articles here reprinted. It is folly to busy
ourselves with discovering new facts about the life of
Spenser, or elucidating the metrical system of Milton,
unless we read the poetry of Milton and Spenser. The best
biographer of Shakespeare is one whose books you put aside
to take down *King Lear*. The best critic of Shelley is he
who makes you go straightway and learn the *Ode to the West
Wind* by heart. The very business of the critic is to be
for ever superseding himself.

That is the sense in which the remark of Rogers may be
applied here. For the judicious reader the new book read
once is an excuse for the old book read again and again for
the twentieth or perhaps the hundredth time. That at any
rate is the common ground taken in the essays here reprinted.
They represent an attempt to use the opportunity provided
by the columns of a newspaper to re-state some of the great
primary positions in literature, and especially in English
poetry. The fundamental truths that lie at the root of
literary criticism, like those that occupy the same position
in morals and politics, are always in danger of finding
a mere acquiescence, respectful but indifferent, where they
should find a vital and understanding acceptance. That is
partly because we change and they do not. We find it
troublesome to be always taking our new bearings with
regard to the fixed stars of the literary firmament, and
though vaguely aware that they are still in their places in
the heavens, we forget them and look up to them no more.
But that way danger lies. For after all it is by them that
we have still to sail, and though a new one is now and then
discovered, the old still remain on their thrones, and the
map of the poetic heaven remains in its great outlines
unchanged. Only we, perhaps, have got round to a new
side of it and do not easily make out where we are. It has
seemed to me that an occasional writer in a newspaper could

hardly use his opportunities better than in making a
modest attempt, for himself and any readers he may have,
to look firmly again at some of these fixed stars, the most
ancient heavens of literature, and try to see once more, as
exactly as individual and newspaper limitations allow,
where they and we stand.

All the essays appeared originally in the Literary Supplement of *The Times*, and I have to thank the proprietors of
that journal for their kindness in allowing me to reprint
them.

Perhaps, as a last word, it may be well to explain here
one small point on which misunderstanding might possibly
arise. The title 'Johnson without Boswell' is that of one
of Sir Walter Raleigh's admirable 'Six Essays on Johnson',
published in 1910. My own article with that title appeared
in *The Times* of August 16, 1907.

J. B.

CONTENTS

POETS AND POETRY

THE FUNCTION OF POETRY [1]

THERE are no questions so eternally worth asking as those
which can never receive an answer. Tennyson said that
nothing worth proving could be proven. So it is with all
the ultimate things which lie at the very heart of our life ; the
unprovable is the root and base alike of faith, and philosophy,
and science. It does not seem likely that the human intelligence will ever discover a final answer to its greatest
questions ; the only certain thing is that it will have signed
its own death-warrant when it gives up asking them. And so
about poetry. When all has been said, poetry must always remain, as Mr. Mackail says in this graceful Inaugural Lecture,
' an invisible thing, a voice, a mystery.' ' No sooner than life
itself will poetry give up its whole secret.' And yet the
day when no one is listening for the voice that will never be
clearly heard, when no one is sounding the depths of the
mystery which will never be plumbed, or giving nights and
days to the search after a secret which will never be revealed,
will not come till civilization has finally surrendered to barbarism, and humanity accepted its own sentence of death.

Mr. Mackail does not go much into these great problems.
Indeed, to be perfectly frank, his Lecture, for the Inaugural
Lecture of a Professor of whom the very highest expectations
were entertained, is a little slight. Its taste and style are of

[1] *The Progress of Poesy.* An Inaugural Lecture, delivered in the
Sheldonian Theatre on the 10th March, 1906. By J. W. Mackail, Professor
of Poetry in the University of Oxford. Clarendon Press. *Wordsworth's
Literary Criticism.* Edited, with an Introduction, by Nowell C. Smith.
Frowde. *Studies in Poetry and Criticism.* By John Churton Collins. Bell.
The Defence of Poesie. By Sir Philip Sidney, Knight. Cambridge
University Press.

course admirable from the first word to the last. But there is not, to tell the truth, a very great deal in it. Most people will have expected from so fine a critic as the author of 'Latin Literature' something more than a graceful analysis of the ode from which he borrows his title, a pleasant account of some of those who have preceded him in his Chair, and a list of Oxford poets. And, indeed, they get something more; they get some acute and interesting, but rather discursive, observations on the nature of poetry and its position at the present moment. But there is nothing in the Lecture that in any way suggests the opening of a new chapter in the history of English criticism. If Mr. Mackail is to be the herald of a new era, it must be his later Lectures that will contain his message.

Still less will anything very new or profound be discovered in the essay on 'The True Functions of Poetry', with which Mr. Churton Collins concludes his recent volume. Here, as elsewhere, Mr. Collins is before all things an amazing memory; and this study, which was apparently written to be delivered as a Lecture, must at least have stimulated any audience capable of poetic stimulus by the splendid passages that are quoted almost on every page. But Mr. Collins's own contribution to the matter, however edifying, is unimportant and even partially false. His theme is the greatness of poetry, and above all its moral and spiritual greatness; he takes as his text Lessing's 'every kind of poetry ought to improve us'. Well, these highest poetic claims cannot be too often vindicated, and Mr. Collins vindicates them with abundant eloquence and inexhaustible powers of illustration. But the strange thing is that he fancies he is a prophet in the wilderness, while in fact, of course, he is at the very centre of things, loudly forcing a door that Wordsworth set wide open a hundred years ago, and no one has since dared to close. This is certain at least as far as the English race is concerned, and it is of England

and English poetry that Mr. Collins appears to be chiefly
thinking. There are exceptions, of course, but the main
and general attitude taken by those who read poetry at this
moment in this country is one learnt in the school of Wordsworth, Coleridge, and Matthew Arnold, the very antipodes
of a disrespectful or frivolous attitude. Nothing could
possibly be further from the truth than such a statement as
this : 'We have so abased the name of poetry, so prostituted
and degraded it by light and frivolous, and even by scan-
dalous and immoral, uses and associations, that, as a name,
it has almost ceased to have any serious significance.' The
human mind and tongue are both free things, and there is
almost nothing that is not somewhere thought and said.
But one would not know where to look for anything stranger
than this astonishing pronouncement coming at the end of
a hundred years during which the moving influences in
English poetry—Wordsworth, Coleridge, Shelley, Tennyson,
Browning, Arnold, all the great ones with the half exceptions of Byron, Keats, and Swinburne—have been men pro-
foundly serious, not to say didactic, the earnest spokesmen of
whole schemes of thought or action which they wished to
get accepted by their countrymen, writers who openly and
deliberately make a large demand on the intellectual, moral,
and even spiritual faculties of those who read them. There
was a day, indeed, when the complaint of Mr. Collins had
some meaning, when poets often were disorderly and undesir-
able persons, and when they were generally thought to be so
whether they were or not. The whole of Sidney's 'Defence
of Poesie' is an attempt to show that poetry is not an idle
and injurious toy, but an aid to good living, private and
political. No one except Mr. Collins now accuses it of
being anything else. But in Sidney's day and long after-
wards, down almost to Wordsworth's day, books of poetry
were looked upon as a dangerous form of temptation lying
in wait for young persons. Who now is afraid that his sons

will spend too much time over poetry? And who regrets any tendency that way if he is so singularly placed as to find it?

The fact is that the danger to poetry is exactly the opposite of what Mr. Collins fancies. Its place as a high thing, 'sage and serious,' is fully acknowledged. Kings, if they chance to read poetry, are no longer thought to disgrace their office, and Tennyson can have Shakespeare before him on his deathbed without any one making allegations of incongruity between the book and the moment. Poets themselves no longer apologize as Pope did, and even Scott, for spending their time so idly as in making verses; they take themselves seriously, and are so taken by others. But that is where the new and most real, however honourable, danger comes in. Poets have entered into their true honours and inheritance only to find that they have lost their popularity. They are now no more popular than other serious things or people. No one finds the appearance of a new poem disorders the working of his household machinery, as unpoetic mothers found when 'Marmion' and 'Childe Harold' appeared. And no novelist would now introduce into his story very commonplace young men and maidens making love by the assistance of recitations from their favourite poets, as is the way of the veracious and unromantic Jane Austen. The question is whether there is not something to regret in that. Neither Scott nor Byron ever quite climbed the heights where the giants of poetry, the true immortals, live. But it is certainly no small thing for a poet to have the power they had of taking their own generation by storm, or carrying it instantaneously captive in a captivity of delight. It was all the world then, not merely people with a turn for literature, who read the last poem that came from the house of Murray. And so in a less degree it was in the eighteenth century. Verse was then regarded, to its own loss as Wordsworth complained, but perhaps also to some people's gain, as one of the fashionable amusements of the time. Everybody read it; everybody recognized that it was a pleasanter and prettier thing than prose. And, as Mr. Mackail points out, it was looked upon as an art which could be taught and learnt like other arts. The Chair which he now holds was founded for the purpose of teaching it; and the first professor laid down as an axiom, the admitted truth of which explains his presence there at all, ' that poetry, like grammar or rhetoric, can be and ought to be taught ': *institutionem et admittere et mereri*. Everybody in those days wrote verses; and, as may be seen in Boswell, the strangest people, quite unknown to the Muses, were spoken of by great critics as ' very good poets '.

Well, it is no doubt a great deliverance to be rid of such a mean conception of poetry as this. But is there no other side to the picture? We may with all our hearts rejoice over the coming of the *vates sacer* ideal of poetry. But need it have been so exclusive as it has tended to become? Is there no place, beside the oracles of the prophets, for more of that poetry which the simplest can follow at once and will at once set themselves to learn by heart? Poets ought surely not to forget that it is their business to win and charm the world: and they need not be quite so scornful as Browning was of the power of tearing an idle man away from his cigar or game of dominoes. This power of sheer fascination is a great and proper part of the poet's function, and we ought not to forget it. Oddly enough, it is Sidney who has the right phrase for it. He talks too much of utility, and he never really understood that the goal of poetry is pleasure: a peculiar pleasure, of course, which uplifts and enlarges, and enriches, and strengthens, but still pleasure. Yet, though the pleasure be for his theory only the sugar to hide the pill of instruction, no one can fall into finer raptures over it than he, as he tells of the poet who ' cometh to you with words set in delightful proportion,

either accompanied with or prepared for the well-enchant-
ing skill of Musicke, and with a tale forsooth he cometh unto
you, with a tale which holdeth children from play and old
men from the chimney corner'. That is the point. Neither
The Excursion nor the *Epipsychidion* will ever do that;
they have a different and perhaps a greater work to do; but
that other work needs to be done, and poetry will not be
fulfilling her whole function till we again have a poet who
can do it.

Her whole function! It is a brave word, far too brave and
far too large for the present occasion. Poetry is a thing as
infinite as life itself, and volumes might be written without
exhausting her attributes. There are some things, however,
that may be said even here. If we are to have an adequate
conception of the work of the poet we must think of the
essence of poetry as being something more universal than
either a force for righteousness or a power of enchanting the
ear. 'The poet', as Wordsworth says in the preface to the
'Lyrical Ballads', one of those admirable critical essays of his
which Mr. Nowell Smith has just reprinted with an excellent
introduction, 'the poet binds together by passion and knowledge the vast empire of human society, as it is spread over
the whole earth and over all time. The objects of the poet's
thoughts are everywhere.... Poetry is the first and last of
all knowledge; it is as immortal as the heart of man.' This
is no flourish of rhetoric; no man was ever less rhetorical
than Wordsworth. 'His writing', as Mr. Nowell Smith
says, 'was, like his character, absolutely sincere'; and, as
he well adds, 'no better instance than Wordsworth's prose
could be found of the value of sincerity in writing—in
other words, of having something which you want to say.'
He wrote these prefaces to plead some causes which lay at
his very heart as a poet and as a man. Some of those pleas
Time has not altogether ratified; but this central one, the
thing that was the very essence of Wordsworth, his faith in

the universality of poetry, has gradually achieved a catholicity of acceptance, ever growing from his day to ours. And whatever else we think about poetry, that is the great doctrine to be clung to. Poetry is the spring which unlocks the hidden life, the essential life, of all that is. Man and Nature are, as Wordsworth always insisted, 'essentially adapted to each other'; and it is poetry, 'the breath and finer spirit of all knowledge,' 'the impassioned expression which is in the countenance of all science,' which is for ever revealing more and more of their affinity. Of that particular work no one, of course, ever did anything like so much as Wordsworth himself; in his hands Man found himself in Nature and Nature in himself. But the revealing of these affinities, great as that task and achievement may be, is only a part, almost an incidental result, of the more universal function of poetry. All attempts to define poetry must obviously come short, as Mr. Mackail says; for, as he adds in what is perhaps the most striking passage in his Lecture, 'such conceptions belong to a scheme of thought based on the idea of a finite machine-made world. Once this conception has given way, as it has done or is doing in every province of human thought, to that of an organic vital process, moving under the control of laws which are themselves vital, organic, progressive, the question of defining poetry, either from abstract principles or by induction of instances, becomes almost meaningless.' The spirit of poetry is a free spirit, blowing where it will, and no one who has ever felt the breath of its wings will care to make the vain attempt to imprison it in a definition. But because it is spirit we can say a little how it acts. Spirit is life, and poetry acts by intensifying all it touches, by raising all to a higher value, by giving life to all. The poet's primrose is a more living thing than the gardener's; the poet's gardener is a more human being than the gardener of the political economist or of the statistician. In the hands of the poet all actions and sensations throb with the redoubled energy of an added life; common things gain joy, common doings beauty. One of the most wonderful of the discoveries of modern science is that of the substance which has the strange property of enabling the human eye to see through very solid and hitherto impenetrable walls of matter. But in another field this is no new discovery, but one of the oldest possessions of the human race. For three thousand years at least, perhaps for much longer, man has enjoyed in poetry the use of a spiritual radium which has enabled him to pierce behind the outer shell and husk of things into their inner life and essential truth. Dull matter has everywhere yielded under its touch, and from the days of Homer to the days of Swinburne there has never been a time when the death of mere fact has not been newborn into the life of poetry.

That is the central thing which includes all the rest. Poetry is to be thought of as a life-giving power, as a radiance of light illuminating all existence, as an energy stimulating all action, as a spirit of beauty giving greatness to all repose. In its presence all things become larger and brighter than they were before. The frenzied agony of Othello, the crimes of Clytemnestra or Macbeth, the weakness of Hamlet, the lawless love of Paolo and Francesca, the fatherly affection of Michael, the passion of Tristram of Lyonnesse, become greater than they were or could be in any other hands; greater, because no longer mere external things seen from outside, clogged and obscured by a clothing of unessential accident and circumstance, but free things, which does not mean things isolated from the influence of the world about them, but things with a true being of their own, into whose secret chambers it is the unique glory of poetry to carry us. Man and nature, nature and art, sea and land, beasts and birds, it is the same everywhere; what comes to us through poetry comes with a higher power of life about it than when it reaches us in any other way.   We love more, we hate, we pity, we wonder, we even understand and know more.   For the simple truth is that we live more ; wherever the breath of poetry passes it leaves behind it the breath of life.

CHAUCER [1]

The French have at present a great interest in the study of 'les langues vivantes', and a great enthusiasm for the labour of translating foreign masterpieces; and so here we have a large volume containing a translation of the whole of the Canterbury Tales of Chaucer, made by a company of scholars, mostly schoolmasters or teachers in the Universities of France. It is not perhaps the exact way which we in England should think the most effective for promoting the study of a mediaeval foreign classic. What would Dante, or Petrarch, or Villon be in a literal prose translation? And how many converts would they make? It would seem obvious that, if the great public is addressed, the one possible method, however unsatisfactory, is a rendering in verse. And, on the other hand, if it is students who are in view, they are certain to desire the original text side by side with the translation. However, Frenchmen must be acknowledged to be the final authority on their own utilities; and what such competent judges as the authors of this volume think likely to be useful to their countrymen must be accepted as being so. In any case, what they have done they have done excellently. The translation is divided line by line, and the lines are marked according to the numbering of Skeat's great Oxford edition; so that, however superior we may think the plan of giving the original opposite the translation and encouraging the student to use the latter only as a crutch, the present book at least does all that its scheme allows.

[1] *Geoffroy Chaucer: Les Contes de Canterbury*. Traduction française. Avec une Introduction et des notes. Par R. Huchon, E. Legouis [and nineteen others]. Paris: Alcan.

The Frenchman who has in his possession the Globe *Chaucer* and this book is in a position to know all that need be known about Chaucer by any one except a specialist. And all the most important part of the knowledge of the specialists is at his disposal. The editors contribute some excellent notes, strictly confined to the two objects of explaining the poet's meaning, and indicating his sources. The text adopted is that of Skeat, from which only a very few departures have been made, and Skeat is also inevitably, as the editors are the first to admit, the principal source of the notes. But, gratefully as they acknowledge their obligations to the Oxford editor, they are no mere servile echoes of his learning. They differ from him from time to time, and, on more than one occasion, may be congratulated on unquestionably putting him right. There can be little doubt, for instance, that in one of the details of the description of the Prioress in the Prologue :—

Full semely after hir mete she raughte—

the rendering which the French give after Skeat in their translation is wrong, and that by which they correct it in their note,

Très décemment elle rotait après son dîner,

is right, however inconsistent with modern notions of graceful behaviour at dinner. Again, they are probably right in changing Skeat's punctuation in lines 413–15 of the Prologue, placing a comma after 'lyk' (this seems to be implied in their note) and substituting a comma for a full stop after 'astronomye'. It is because he was 'grounded in astronomye' that the Doctor

kepte his pacient a ful greet del
In houres, by his magik naturel.

Once more they seem to be right in another afterthought introduced into the additional notes at the end of the book, one which suggests that the right meaning of line 602—

Ther coude no man bringe him in arrerage—

is not, as Skeat thought, 'no man could prove him to be
in arrears,' but 'no man could make him late in getting
in his money'. This seems to be confirmed by the subsequent lines about the impossibility of deceiving him by
any tricks.

These illustrations will be enough to show that the work
of the French editors is the work of scholars, men who have
learned in the best school of Chaucerian knowledge, but
have retained their own rights of judgement and show themselves fit to use it. But the notes are after all very few,
however excellent; they occupy probably less than a fiftieth
part of the letterpress of the book. The bulk of the work
is the translation, in strictly literal prose except a very few
tales which are rendered in unrhymed verse, or, in the
editors' own phrase, *lignes parisyllabiques.*

The part which has received the most careful revision,
they tell us, is the Prologue, undoubtedly the most difficult,
as well as the most important, part of the poem. A comparison of the rendering of the latter half of this with the
original does not reveal many mistranslations, and none
of importance. 'To drawen folk to heven by fairnesse' is
probably not perfectly rendered by 'mener les gens au ciel
par la droiture'; for 'fairnesse' surely means more than
'honesty'. Is not its idea something more like St. Paul's
'whatsoever things are lovely'? It is not the uprightness
of the Parson which is his leading characteristic, but the
evangelical beauty of his temper and life. Again, 'il ne
cherchait ni honneurs ni dignités' does not give the right
notion of

He wayted after no pompe and reverence,

which surely refers to his humility of intercourse with his
people, not to his freedom from ecclesiastical ambition.

It may, perhaps, be desirable to give a specimen of the
translation. Here are lines 751-75:—

Un fort digne homme était notre hôte à tout prendre,
fait pour être majordome d'une salle de festin.
C'était un homme corpulent, aux yeux brillants ;
de plus beau bourgeois il n'en est point dans Cheap-
    side :
le verbe hardi, et sage, et bien instruit ;
et de ce qui fait l'homme rien certes ne lui manquait.
D'ailleurs c'était aussi un bon vivant,
et après souper il se met à plaisanter,
et tint joyeux devis entre autres choses,
lorsque nous eûmes réglé notre compte,
et dit : ' Eh bien, Messeigneurs, en vérité,
vous êtes pour moi de tout cœur les bienvenus ;
car sur ma foi si je ne dois mentir,
je n'ai vu de cette année si joyeuse compagnie
réunie en cette auberge, qu'à présent.
Volontiers je vous mettrais en joie, si je savais com-
    ment ;
et d'un amusement je viens de m'aviser
qui vous égayera, et ne vous coûtera rien.
Vous allez à Canterbury ; Dieu vous aide !
Le bienheureux martyr vous récompense !
et j'en suis sûr, le long du chemin,
vous voulez vous dire des contes, et vous réjouir ;
car vraiment, il n'est point d'agrément ni de joie
à chevaucher par les chemins muet comme pierre ;
Et c'est pourquoi je veux vous amuser,
comme je l'ai dit, et vous donner quelque plaisir.'

How much impression this can give of the light-tripping
gaiety of Chaucer only a Frenchman who knows English
very well can say; probably not very much. Chaucer's
manner of expressing himself can only be partly retained,
and the pleasant movement of his verse is necessarily lost
altogether. But at least the translators have given their
countrymen a useful companion to guide and help them
in reading Chaucer. The rendering, it will be seen, is
very careful and accurate. Everything is there but the
bloom of the verse; and the reader knows exactly what
Chaucer said, if that can ever be known by those who do
not know how he said it. Only one expression, perhaps,
can be disputed. ' Eek thereto he was right a mery man '

is given, one thinks, a suggestion not in the original by
'C'était aussi un bon vivant'. The phrase 'bon vivant'
apparently means in modern French what we mean by it
when we borrow it in English; and in Chaucer's 'mery
man' there is no direct allusion to the pleasures of the
table.

But these are, after all, very small points. They cannot
be said to detract seriously from the merit of the service
which the authors of this book have rendered to France.
They have given a real impetus to the study of one of the
sanest, brightest, and most lovable of poets. We are apt
to think that the French are stronger in wit than in humour.
But, whether that be so or not, they have, at least, more
than once shown a very warm appreciation of humour.
The unique place of affection which they have always kept
in their hearts for their own delightful La Fontaine is
enough to show that in France, as elsewhere, humour does
not fail to win a kind of love sought for in vain by more
brilliant gifts and graces; and there is more than one
point of resemblance between La Fontaine and Chaucer. It
is not only a question of manner, though there the parallel
is so marked that M. Legouis, in his most suggestive introduction to the translation, well applies to Chaucer the line
which describes the most winning of La Fontaine's peculiarities:

Ses nonchalances sont ses plus grands artifices.

But it goes deeper than that. The La Fontaine of the
Contes, it is true, remains at the stage in poetry which
it was Chaucer's special business to supersede. But the
La Fontaine of the *Fables* performs exactly the same magical
act of transformation on the dull little moralities of Phaedrus,
or whoever it may be, as Chaucer performs on the authors
from whom he takes his material. A critic who did not
mind exaggeration might call it a transformation out of
death into life. In each case what was a mere story, a

mere string of incidents calculated to amuse or to instruct,
becomes a living comedy of manners. The main interest is
transferred from the machinery of the plot to the character
of the actors. Professor Vaughan has lately been telling us
that this has been historically the line of progress of the
drama. Chaucer marks the turning-point of the same
process in the case of the mediaeval tale. His two great
achievements were, first, the variety of tone and manner
which he secured for the mediaeval fashion of a collection of
tales by his brilliant idea of taking a party of pilgrims as his
spokesmen. Nothing else could have so naturally brought
together all ranks of society, and so enabled all attitudes
towards human life to find expression in the scheme of the
poem, in a way quite impossible, for instance, to the elegant
exclusiveness of the contemporary *Decamerone*. The other
achievement was still more fundamental. As M. Legouis
says admirably, 'tandis que Boccace ne dépasse guère le
tableau de mœurs, Chaucer s'avance progressivement vers
l'étude des caractères. . . . Chez lui l'intrigue, l'anecdote
initiale, qui fut le tout du fabliau, et qui reste le principal
dans Boccace, passe à l'arrière-plan, s'efface, n'est plus guère
qu'un prétexte.' And then he goes on to say that you
cannot transfer the weight to character in this way without
destroying the balance of the old *conte* altogether.
Directly you have truth of character-painting you have
an inevitable awakening of sympathy. There is no real
knowledge without something like a kind of love in these
things. And so you have a divided interest. The old
fabliau in which you merely laugh at the deluded husband
is transformed into Chaucer's *Merchant's Tale*, where there
are the beginnings of a sympathy for the old cheated
January. The mere story of *The Cock and the Fox* is en-
riched by all the humour and life of the *Nonne Preste's Tale*.
Or, to go again to La Fontaine, the drily unsympathetic
little morality of *The Ant and the Grasshopper* becomes the

first of the new fables, asking our sympathies quite as much for the *Cigale* as for the *Fourmi*. The 'comédie simple', in fact, so far as it was ever entitled to the great name of comedy at all, has become something at once more human and more complex, what M. Legouis calls 'le drame sans parti pris exclusif, oscillant entre le rire et la pitié'. That is the transformation you experience when you pass from the fable of Phaedrus to the fable of La Fontaine, or, as M. Legouis says, from the *Poirier enchanté* of Boccaccio, (it is the ninth story of the seventh day of the *Decameron*), to the *Merchant's Tale* as told by Chaucer.

That is a great achievement, and to have accomplished it is Chaucer's most essential glory. The man who, more than any one else, took the decisive step on the journey which has carried humanity from the *Arabian Nights* to the great novels of the nineteenth century, one might almost have said to *Hamlet* and *Macbeth*, is a man whose fame cannot be an affair of purely national interest. M. Legouis does, perhaps, less than justice to the serious side of his genius. He is not negligible as a 'poète de la piété, de la chevalerie, ou du sentiment' because the sources of nearly all his serious poetry are easily traceable. If that were so, it would be quite arguable that Shakespeare was negligible as a dramatist. Still, there is no doubt that Chaucer's strength lies chiefly in things of a lighter cast. He was apparently a man of a practical turn of mind, with no inclination towards high spiritual adventures of any kind. He has the easy pleasantness of one who most certainly enjoys living his own life, but also, and almost equally, enjoys looking on at the lives of other people. Man as man interests him, and woman as woman. He observes, and notes and remembers, but scarcely ever judges. Like Shakespeare he has been inside everybody, and consequently has found some element of a good fellow even in the dirtiest scoundrel who comes in his way. Even

Shakespeare has not a more universal tolerance. Which
does he depict with the greater pleasure, the poor Parson
or the Wife of Bath? Who knows? But then who knows
whether Shakespeare took as much pleasure in Desdemona
as in Falstaff? Chaucer, at any rate, cannot be entirely
hostile to any of his creatures. No one ever had a better
right to take *humani nihil* for his motto. He is full of
liking for his most unmonastic Monk, and not without
appreciation of the accomplishments of his rascally Friar.
Even the universally detested Pardoner and Somnour
arouse nothing approaching indignation in him. They are
part of the human comedy; and, when all the worst of
them has been set down, not at all in malice, it remains
true that one of them is 'in chirche a noble ecclesiaste',
and that you cannot anywhere find a 'bettre felawe' than
the other.

What a long way we have travelled here from the ancient
facit indignatio versus! What a world away we are from
the only other great poet of the Middle Age! There are
heights in human things that Chaucer never tried to climb,
depths that he could not fathom. For Dante, life was a
journey from earth through Purgatory to Heaven, and the
only thing that greatly mattered was reaching the goal.
For Chaucer, whatever fine things he, like any other man of
imagination in the Middle Age, could say of Heaven or Hell,
the thought of the greatness of the goal was far less present
than that of the agreeableness of the journey. He found
his way through this delightful earth pleasant enough to
occupy nearly all his attention; and what fills his mind, and
therefore his poetry, is the pleasant company that is to be
met with on the road, the fair creations of Art and of Nature
that are to be seen as one passes along it, the variety, the
curiousness, the perpetual and unfailing fascination, of all
the diverse sights and sounds, ways and doings, livings,
lovings, and dyings that make up the daily spectacle

provided unceasingly for a man of open eyes by the world
of plant and flower, of beast and bird, above all, of man and
woman, that is about him on every side. That is Chaucer,
the wide-minded man rather than the profound, the man of
quick sympathies rather than of deep heart, very lovable,
very human, of our own flesh and blood, not of some high
prophetic temper like Dante, not a creature of pure spirit,
ethereal and enskied, like Shelley. The French will do well
to get acquainted with him. With one side of them, indeed
—the 'red fool fury' that made the Revolution and the
Commune, the declamatory rhetoric that is always posturing
and beating the air and never perceiving its own ridiculous-
ness—Chaucer has nothing at all in common. His good
sense and good temper, his middling wisdom, above all his
easy habit of returning upon himself the moment he is
tempted to go too far in any direction, are the very opposite
of the things that found their culmination in Victor Hugo.
But there is another strain in the temperament of France.
Jacques Bonhomme reappears as surely, generation after
generation, in that pleasant land as his rival, the violent
and loud-mouthed ' chercheur de gros mots '. The very Com-
munards who tried to burn the Louvre and were ready to
kill half Paris and ruin the rest in pursuit of their impracti-
cable crudities were the compatriots and contemporaries of
some millions of sensible peasants, who had no desire to kill
anybody or burn anything so long as they were allowed to
till their land and eat the fruits of it. And they were also
the compatriots of people who had perfected, more than it
has ever been perfected elsewhere, the art of living agreeably
to oneself and to one's neighbours. With that other France,
the cheerful and sensible France, making the best of plain
things when Fortune gives no more, but not forgetting to
take delighted possession of all the wise, pleasant, and
beautiful things that come from her hand whenever she is
in more liberal mood, Chaucer is in closest kinship. It will

understand him at once, and will at once recognize in him a kindred spirit. For he, too, might well have said of himself, with *Polyphile*—

> J'aime le jeu, l'amour, les livres, la musique,
> La ville et la campagne, enfin tout: il n'est rien
> Qui ne me soit souverain bien;

and Frenchmen who are of that wise temper will be grateful to M. Legouis and his colleagues for helping them to know him, and will gladly welcome him to his fit place in the company of poets that groups itself round Molière and La Fontaine.

SIR PHILIP SIDNEY [1]

OF all the English poets none has a fame so independent
of his poetry as Sidney. Other poets—Milton, for instance,
and Marvell—have played as great or a greater part in the
life of their country; but their lives had not the grace, nor
their deaths the glory, of the life and death of Sidney.
His life was mainly, at least in appearance, the most futile
and barren that a man can choose, that of a courtier; yet
he managed so to tread that trivial stage that his fellow-
actors in the piece discovered to their surprise that there
was a part in it for the wise man, the hero, and the saint.
He died in one of the most inglorious of English military
exploits; but he so died that he has buried its shame
in the eternity of his nobleness. No one ever lived more
loved or died more lamented. *Tu Marcellus eris.* That
was the feeling of all England and of many high hearts
outside England, when the news of Zutphen came. *Mani-
bus date lilia plenis.* All the poets did that—Constable
in a noble sonnet, Raleigh in a long 'epitaph' fuller of
thought and matter and the sorrow of admiration than of
poetry; and the greatest of them, the one who had paid
Sidney perhaps the finest compliment even he ever received
by calling himself 'the southern shepherd's boy', Spenser,
who wished to be thought Sidney's scholar and pupil,
poured out his grief again and again for his country's loss
and his own.

[1] *The Poems of Sir Philip Sidney.* Edited, with an Introduction, by
John Drinkwater. The Muses' Library: Routledge.

O noble spirit! live there ever blest.
The world's late wonder, and the heaven's new joy:
Live ever there, and leave me here distrest
With mortal cares and cumbrous world's annoy;
But where thou dost that happiness enjoy
Bid me, O! bid me quickly come to thee,
That happy there I may thee always see.

'The world's late wonder, and the heaven's new joy'—
that was not a mere phrase of compliment, as it so easily
might have been; the words, coming from Spenser's mouth
and applied to Sidney, meant exactly what they said, what
the poet sincerely felt. And more than the poet, more
even than that Elizabethan world which first wept over
Sidney's death. It has been the feeling, in some degree,
of all sensitive spirits from that day till now. For the
service of the State, for the new hopes of literature, for a
greater thing than either, human life itself, the picture and
growth of it as a thing of beauty and perfection, the death
of Sidney at the age of thirty-two was one of the tragedies
of history. It is one of those events of which, after three
hundred years, we are still unable to read without thinking
of what might have been. Such force is there in a great
name when it is the symbol of so many fair things as were
joined together in Sidney; noble birth, a high part to play,
and a great stage to play it on; this world and all the glory
of it; gifts, great enough to make the memory of another
man, and yet, in this case, only the setting of things much
brighter and more precious; wisdom beyond the young
years, virtue walking erect in very slippery places, a burn-
ing love of country shining bright in a world of intrigue;
and, in an age still struggling out of barbarism, the divine
gift of poetry.

Sidney's poetry, like everything else about him, is perhaps greater in a certain charm of presence and promise
than in actual performance. But he is still of real, not
merely of historical, importance. The business of English

poetry after the death of Chaucer was to get back to his
ease, his metrical power, his large and human naturalness,
his beauty of speech and form; and it took about two
hundred years to do it. In that long journey Surrey and
Wyatt represent the first important stage and Sidney the
second. The first may have been the more difficult; but
that the second carried us a good deal further than the first
may be seen at once by putting Surrey's best sonnets side
by side with Sidney's. There is a certain strength in the
Epitaph on Clere which Sidney never acquired; and
Sidney himself never wrote a lovelier line than

Aye me! whilst life did last that league was tender.

But Sidney would have been scarcely more likely than
Waller or Pope to let such a rugged verse as

Clere, of the Count of Cleremont, thou hight,

be circulated with his name attached to it. In the forty
years or so that lie between them had come a new beauty
of language and a new mastery of rhythm of which Sidney
was the first example and of which he must retain the
credit, however soon and however completely his achievements were eclipsed by Spenser and a greater even than
Spenser. Between Chaucer and Sidney there is no English poetry either of such human and rational outlook upon
life or of such fine workmanship as the *Astrophel and
Stella* Sonnets. They still, it is true, abound in the forced
fancies which were partly an inheritance from the Middle
Age, and partly a new irrationality of that very Renaissance which claimed to bring, and did bring, a purifying
fire of reason into so many fields of human activity. But
irritated or wearied as we may easily be by such tiresome
affectations as the 'roses gules' on the 'silver field' of
Stella's face, we very soon become aware that that is not
Sidney; it is only the fashion of his time, from which no
man entirely escapes. The true Sidney, the Sidney who

was a new and permanent star in our poetical heaven, is
not in things of that sort, over-frequent as they are, but
rather in such things as—

> True that true beauty Virtue is indeed,
> Whereof this beauty can be but a shade
> Which elements with mortal mixture breed.
> True, that on earth we are but pilgrims made,
> And should in soul up to our country move ;
> True, and yet true that I must Stella love.

or the wonderful openings of his two most famous sonnets :—

> With how sad steps, O Moon, thou climb'st the skies

and

> Come, Sleep! O Sleep, the certain knot of peace,
> The baiting-place of wit, the balm of woe,

where we are not surprised to find that we have foretastes
of Shelley and Shakespeare ; or such lines, fit to hold their
place in any ripest poetry of all the world, as—

> And yet amid all fears a hope there is

or

> And Love doth hold my hand and makes me write

or

> And Humbleness grows one with Majesty,

or that Shakespearian

> Gone is the winter of my misery.

This is the poetry which Mr. Drinkwater makes more
accessible by his handy little volume. He prefaces it with
two introductions, a biographical and a critical ; both com-
petently and sensibly done, telling the plain reader all he
need know about the man and the poet. On the thorny
and controversial question of the relation in which the
poet's sonnets stand to the facts of his life, the relation of
Astrophel and Stella to Philip Sidney and Penelope Deve-
reux, he takes, if we may dare to brave some distinguished
critics enough to say so, the only line that is possible to a
man who knows what poetry is. Dante and Beatrice,

Petrarch and Laura, Sidney and Stella, Shelley and Emilia
Viviani, Shakespeare and the mysterious youth—these are
not fictions, still less are they facts. They are poetry,
which is neither fiction nor fact but truth. To suppose
that the convincing intensity of the *Vita Nuova* or the
sonnets of Sidney or Shakespeare proves that they are
newspaper biographies of their subjects is simply to show
that the critic does not understand the nature of poetry.
To suppose that the slightness, coldness, and bareness of
the relations of the lovers in actual fact, so far as we know
them, prove that the poems are mere fictions, is simply
to make the same mistake from the opposite side. Great
poets do not live in a vacuum ; they have their eyes and
hands on life, their own life and the lives of others. The
poet finds in life the stuff of his work ; but he never leaves
it as he finds it. He touches nothing without transfiguring
it, recreating it, giving it new birth; and only one who
should have as great a genius for seeing prose in poetry as
the poet has for seeing poetry in prose could rediscover
the facts out of a reading of the poems. Sidney was in love
' with an ideal of his own ', as Mr. Drinkwater says, and he
chose to clothe Penelope Rich with it. How much of it
actually belonged to her we can no more tell now than we
can travel back from Michael Angelo's Lorenzo dei Medici
to the actual Duke of Urbino.

It is unfortunate that Mr. Drinkwater's editing is not on
a level with his two introductions. He has allowed far more
misprints and mistakes to slip through than should be
excused even in a popular reprint of this sort. To give
one instance only, the word ' draught ' in Sonnet 38 is
puzzling enough to the ordinary reader without being mis-
spelt ' drought ', which simply renders it entirely unintelligible. Nor can he be congratulated upon his few notes.
Such notes as that on the thirty-ninth sonnet, where he
goes out of his way to mention Grosart's ridiculous notion

that there is a play on 'sub rosa' in the words 'a rosy garland', and only puts it aside to suggest that the words refer to 'the light of imagination in the mind', are the very reverse of helpful. When the poet wrote 'rosy garland' he meant what he said and nothing else, just as he did when he wrote 'smooth pillows' or 'sweetest bed'.

But these are small matters, and the reason for this little book's existence is not notes, or even introductions, but Sidney himself. Those who buy it will do so because they want to have *Astrophel and Stella* to put in their pockets. And there will always be people who want to do that as long as English poetry has readers. For Sidney has some claim to be considered the first of our poets to use the English language in its permanent and final shape. Chaucer, who was born two hundred years before him, could anticipate it by flashes of genius, could help powerfully to create it; but he could not, in the nature of things, write it continuously. Spenser, who was born two years before him, may almost be said to have carefully avoided doing so. But in Sidney we come, not occasionally but constantly. upon poetry that could not be accused of any affectation of archaism if it were written to-day.

I never drank of Aganippe well,
Nor ever did in shade of Tempe sit,
And Muses scorn with vulgar brains to dwell;
Poor layman I, for sacred rites unfit.
Some do I hear of poets' fury tell,
But (God wot) wot not what they mean by it;
And, this I swear by blackest brook of hell,
I am no pick-purse of another's wit.
How falls it then that with so smooth an ease
My thoughts I speak; and what I speak doth flow
In verse, and that my verse best wits doth please?
Guess we the cause! What, is it thus? Fie, no.
Or so? Much less. How then? Sure thus it is,
My lips are sweet, inspired with Stella's kiss.

There is not a word here which poets do not use to-day.

Sidney attained at one stroke what was denied to the age of Chaucer and left unsought by the archaism of Spenser, the English that was coming and was to remain the mature and perfect language of English poetry. Of course he does not give the whole; the whole was to include, for instance, large contributions from Spenser, of whom so much was almost immediately rejected. But all Sidney gave has been kept. His English was the English of the seventeenth and eighteenth centuries, and it is still ours. That is seen even more clearly in some of the songs than in the sonnets. And it is good to have an excuse for reminding people that *Astrophel and Stella* is a book not only of sonnets but of songs. Take this, for example :—

> But when their tongues could not speak,
> Love itself did silence break;
> Love did set his lips asunder
> Thus to speak in love and wonder.
>
> 'Stella, sovereign of my joy,
> Fair triumpher of annoy:
> Stella, star of heavenly fire,
> Stella, loadstar of desire,
>
> 'Stella in whose shining eyes
> Are the lights of Cupid's skies:
> Whose beams when they once are darted,
> Love therewith is straight imparted.
>
> 'Stella, whose voice, when it speaks
> Senses all asunder breaks:
> Stella, whose voice when it singeth,
> Angels to acquaintance bringeth.

In poetic quality, pretty as it is, this seems to live on the surface of things when compared with the best sonnets; and of course the imaginative atmosphere belongs, in part at any rate, to a generation that was passing away. But the language does not; nor the ease and spontaneity of movement. They look on to Herrick and Waller, and even to Prior and Phillips.

But there is more in Sidney than merely technical achievement. He was a real poet. Whether if he had lived he would have been one of our great poets it is impossible now to say. Probably not. To be that demands more of a man than he—with his eyes fixed on great action in the field of politics and religion—would ever have given. Only Milton could greatly serve two masters; and he, besides being Milton, knew from the first which it was his peculiar call to serve; and after a brief desertion, for a special end, faithfully returned to his post. But what Sidney actually did in his few years, and in spite of his divided interests, is enough to give him a high place, a place among the poets who live in their own right, and not by grace of historical considerations. He was the perfect flower of that singular society in which, to use language which would not have seemed to it in the least priggish, it was the admitted aim of a gentleman to learn and practise both the intellectual and the moral virtues. Spenser described it as a man of letters and as an artist. Sidney was within it, was himself its model and hero. And he brought the lofty seriousness of its ideal, its unfaltering conviction that life is a thing with a meaning, into his poetry with such fine instinct as to make of a series of love sonnets a school not merely of art and language but of manners and of life. They are not written for edification, as so much of Spenser is, and their language is not primarily the language of edification. But take it at its most unrestrained phase, take it where in appearance the poet abandons himself most unreservedly to his passion, and is it, we ask, an unedifying effect that it produces even there? If a poet have as high a soul as Sophocles, said Goethe, he will produce a moral effect whatever he does. Here is what is, perhaps, Sidney's most passionate sonnet; we will leave it to give its own answer as to the effect it produces :—

No more, my dear, no more these counsels try;
O give my passions leave to run their race;
Let Fortune lay on me her worst disgrace;
Let folk o'ercharged with brain against me cry;
Let clouds bedim my face, break in mine eye:
Let me no steps but of lost labour trace;
Let all the earth with scorn recount my case—
But do not will me from my love to fly.
I do not envy Aristotle's wit,
Nor do aspire to Caesar's bleeding fame;
Nor aught do care though some above me sit;
Nor hope nor wish another course to frame,
But that which once may win thy cruel heart;
Thou art my wit and thou my virtue art.

ALEXANDER HUME [1]

How many of us have so much as heard of Alexander Hume? The judicious lover of poetry, learning late by many disappointments, has no very high anticipations when he comes upon these erudite reprints provided for him by societies that too often confuse archaeology with literature, and think doggerel becomes poetry by having been three hundred years contentedly forgotten. But he may venture hopefully on this last publication by the Scottish Text Society. Alexander Hume was a true poet and an interesting man, and he has found in Mr. Lawson a most conscientious, learned, modest, and wholly admirable editor. Almost too modest, indeed; for he is the very opposite of most of those who discover or rediscover ancient worthies for us, and tends rather to under-rate than to over-rate his hero's rank and quality. It is a most refreshing contrast to the tone of such editors as, for instance, the late Mr. Grosart, whose immense learning and unwearied industry were sadly counterbalanced by a lack of critical capacity which led him to see a pearl of great price in every pebble he picked up on an Elizabethan field. Hume, on the other hand, is all, and more than all, Mr. Lawson claims for him; and the Scottish Text Society would have deserved well of the republic of letters if this volume were its solitary achievement. Here is the man, as Mr. Lawson sums him up for us; it is the portrait of one who would have been worth looking at, if he had never created a line of poetry :—

[1] *The Poems of Alexander Hume* (? 1557-1609). Edited from the text of Waldegrave (1599), with Notes, Appendices, and Glossary, by Alexander Lawson, Berry Professor of English Literature in the University of St. Andrews. Scottish Text Society. Blackwood.

He comes before us as somewhat severe, but always pure
in purpose, clear in thought, and elevated in aspiration—
a forgotten Father of the National Church who has incon-
testable claims to reverence, because he fought stoutly a
good fight, and because, amid many difficulties and sore
discouragements, he finished a course in which he forfeited
no claim either to wisdom or to beauty of soul. His life
was no tranquil summer day. It had its sunshine, and
shower, and tempest; but when the 'gloaming' came, ere
the sun went wholly out of sight, it left such streaks of
purple and scarlet in the sky that we still look back with
pleasure.

There is Alexander Hume, a gentleman who saw more in
the Reformation than a mere opportunity of plunder, a
clergyman who saw more in it than antiprelacy and pre-
destination, a poet who could put it gently aside and set
himself to sing the praises of a summer day.

Born about 1557 of a good stock, of which were after-
wards to come three other names of some note—Patrick
Hume, Milton's first editor, John, the author of *Douglas*,
and the great David, the philosopher,—our Alexander Hume
studied first, probably, at St. Andrews, and then, certainly,
four years in France; and brought from there, no doubt,
a certain geniality, a sense of life and delight in beauty
which might easily have deserted him in his later days of
controversy, but never quite did. Returning to Scotland
about 1580 he tried the lawyer's life first, and then, strangely
enough, the courtier's; but, too sensitive, impatient, and
sincere to find either endurable, he gets through the next
years as well as he may (better for us than for himself, for
it was at this time that his poems were written), till in 1597
he was admitted minister of Logie, not far from Stirling.
There he lived his remaining years, writing no more verse,
but seeing what he had already written published by Waldegrave in 1599. He held a conspicuous position among the
clergy, and his life at Logie was naturally occupied chiefly

with ministerial duties and Church controversies. He died
on December 4, 1609.

Mr. Lawson says of him that his 'work falls to be considered almost wholly in two aspects. He is a poet and he
is a Churchman. In neither sphere is he important, but in
each he is characteristic and eminently individual.' Well,
it is perhaps a question of words, but some of us might be
inclined to consider that to be 'characteristic and eminently
individual' was the gift of gifts, at least in letters, and
carried importance with it as a matter of course. In any
case, Hume was everywhere himself and no one else, a man
and not an echo. How beautifully alone he stands, for
instance, in his book of *Christian Precepts*, calling back his
countrymen, if he could, from controversial pre-occupations
to the spiritual life, from a religion dry, external, political,
intellectual, to one of inwardness, sanctity, and peace. To
seem to echo *The Imitation* was, in that day, as original
a thing as a Scotch minister could accomplish; and Hume
achieved it, in the best sense. The finest of his precepts
might be bound up with *The Imitation* and not seem out of
place; these, for instance, and such as these :—

Learn to be sad, silent, sober, and sanctified: having thy
mind ever lifted upward, and pansing (i. e. thinking) on
heavenly things, and not on earthly and base things.

To make thee charitable towards all men, think that they
with whom thou hast to do are of the number of the children
of God. And when thou speakest of the dead, think that
they are in Christ's Kingdom, and this will make thee bridle
thy tongue.

Panse (i. e. think) deeply, and consider with thyself what
kind of thing Eternity is.

This little collection of Precepts should certainly be issued
by itself as a book of practical devotion. There are few of
finer quality in existence.

But to come to Hume's poetry. There is not a great deal
of it, and all there is, with two partial exceptions, is of a

religious cast; not the kind of poetry that has often shown much power of interesting posterity. But it is our fault, not Hume's, if he has not been remembered. Take him at his best, and he has a splendour which makes us think of Milton's visions of Heaven, and a spiritual beauty which suggests his great English contemporary, Spenser. Will any one think this extravagant praise, after reading these noble stanzas from the *Consolation to his Sorrowful Soul*? It seems best to retain the spelling of the original.

> The angels sall with singing thee convoy,
> Throw aire and fire vp to the heauens sa bright,
> Where thou sall dwell in blis and perfite ioy,
> With happie sauls and messengers of light,
> Free from the thoughts and sorrowes of the night,
> Uoide of all care, calamitie, and feare.
> For of the Lord thou sall inioy the sight,
> In whome all grace, and pleasour sall appeare.
> With Christ thy head thou happie sall remaine,
> To iudge the dead while he returne againe.
>
> O happie death to life the readie way,
> The ende of greefe, and salue of sorrowes all,
> O pleasant sleepe, thy paines they are bot play;
> Thy coup is sweete, although it taste of gall:
> Thou brings the bound and wretched out of thrall,
> Within the port sure from the stormie blast.
> For after death na mischiefe may befall,
> Bot wo, wan-chance, and perrels all are past.
> Of kindely death nane suld affraied be,
> Bot sick as hope for na felicitie.
>
> The day sall come when all the planets seauen,
> Sall lose their light, and mightie influence,
> The glistering starnis, and powers of the heauen,
> Their force sall faile, and haill magnificence,
> The saincts of God sall suffer violence,
> The common course of mortall things sall stay,
> The liuely word sall get na audience,
> For pittie, love, and lawtie (i. e. loyalty) sall decay:
> Then sall the Sonne of man be sene descend,
> Quhilk to all things sall put a finall ende.

Is it an extravagance to say that there is a foretaste of

Milton in the first and third of the stanzas? And will it
be easily believed that the second was written before, and
not after, the appearance of the wonderful lines Spenser
puts so strangely into the mouth of the villain Despair?—

> What if some little pain the passage have,
> That makes frail flesh to fear the bitter wave,
> Is not short pain well borne, that brings long ease,
> And lays the soul to sleep in quiet grave?
> Sleep after toil, port after stormy seas,
> Ease after war, death after life, does greatly please.

But before looking at this, most readers will turn to the
Triumph of the Lord, written in October, 1589, in celebra-
tion of the defeat of the Spanish Armada. It is curiously
characteristic of its day, with its mixture of a long description of a Roman triumph borrowed from Plutarch, and a
Song of the Lord's Soldiers which is, in the main, a recital
of the story of Israel. But it is not only the Elizabethan
incongruity which it exhibits. Where, except among the
very great men, shall we find a nobler example of the
Elizabethan spaciousness, the Elizabethan largeness of utterance, than in such lines as these:—

> Bot quha pretends the puissance to declare,
> Right as it is, or enters to compare
> The glore of God with that of mortall men,
> Sall tyne bot time, and tyre his painefull pen.
> Als far as light the darknes dois deface
> Or hell is from the highest holy place,
> Als far as slaves are from the stait of Kings,
> Or widdring weids from euerlasting thinges:
> Als far His might surmounts the might of man,
> His pompe and pride, and all the craft he can.

But even more attractive than these is the poem called
Of the Day Estivall. It would be a pleasure to quote
every word of it; style, metre, fancy, loving observation
of man and nature, all show the poet at his very best,
and make this 'summer day' a thing which Stevenson must

have learnt by heart, if he ever came across it.   It begins,
of course, as it ends, with a word of piety :—

> O Perfite light, quhilk schaid away
> The darkenes from the light,
> And set a ruler ou'r the day
> Ane vther ou'r the night.
>
> Thy glorie, when the day foorth flies,
> Mair viuely dois appeare
> Nor at midday vnto our eyes
> The shining Sun is cleare.

Then follows the picture of the summer dawn and the early
notes of the birds : and then :—

> Up braids the carefull husbandman,
> His cornes and vines to see,
> And euerie tymous artisan
> In buith worke busilie.
>
> . . . .
>
> The passenger from perrels sure,
> Gangs gladly foorth the way ;
> Briefe, everie liuing creature
> Takes comfort of the day.
>
> . . . .
>
> The time sa tranquill is and still,
> That na where sall ye find,
> Saife on ane high and barren hill,
> Ane aire of peeping wind.
>
> All trees and simples great and small,
> That balmie leife do beir,
> Nor thay were painted on a wall,
> Na mair they moue or steir.
>
> Calme is the deepe and purpour se,
> Yee smuther nor the sand,
> The wals that woltring wont to be
> Are stable like the land.

Then follows the picture of the heat of noon, much of this
and other parts of the poem being clearly founded on
Hume's memories of France.

The labowrers that timellie raise,
All wearie faint and weake:
For heate downe to their houses gais
Noone-meate and sleepe to take.

. . . . .

Sume plucks the honie plowm and peare,
The cherrie and the pesche,
Some likes the reamand (i. e. foaming) London beare,
The bodie to refresh.

The cooler afternoon follows, and

Furth fairis the flocks to seeke their fude,
On euerie hill and plaine,
Ilk labourer as he thinks gude
Steppes to his turne again.

. . . .

Great is the calm: for euerie quhair
The wind is sitten downe,
The reik (i. e. smoke) thrawes right vp in the air,
From euerie towre and towne.

And then the evening:—

What pleasour were to walke and see
Endlang a riuer cleare,
The perfite forme of euerie tree
Within the deepe appeare?

. . . . . .

And, last, the home-coming—

Throw all the land great is the gild (i. e. clamour)
Of rustik folks that crie,
Of bleiting sheepe fra they be fild,
Of calues and rowting ky.

All labourers drawes hame at even,
And can till vther say,
Thankes to the gracious God of heauen,
Quhilk send this summer day.

If Hume had written nothing but this most delightful
poem, he would deserve a special place in the hearts of all
who have felt how good it is to be alive in June. The
surprises of literature are as endless as those of life. Who

would have looked to an old Presbyterian minister, doing valiant business for the Kirk in controversy with an English Bishop, to be the man to paint the liveliest picture of the beauty, calm, and human blessedness that a summer's day brings always to fit receivers, now as then, then as now?

SPENSER [1]

THE *Faery Queen* is a long poem, and many people will
not read long poems. In Spenser's case, then, even more
than in others, a selection has a useful part to play. Here
we have in a small and handy shape a good deal of his
most perfect poetry, the *Epithalamion*, of course, the *Hymn
of Heavenly Beauty*, some fine fragments of the *Ruins of
Time* and the *Tears of the Muses*, the best months of the
Shepherd's Calendar, and some dozen noble episodes from
the *Faery Queen*. If any one takes up this book as his first
sight of Spenser, and has not begun to want a complete
Spenser long before he has finished it, he has mistaken his
vocation. Whatever else he was meant for, he was not meant
to be a reader of poetry. For it is hardly too much to say
that in this little volume is contained a kind of quintessence
of all that is most poetic in poetry. That was really Spenser's
great gift. He is ' our sage and serious Spenser '—much more
so than Mr. Yeats understands—but he is also and before
all things the most poetic of poets. Poetry may be so many
things ; it may be instructive, edifying, inspiring, startling,
amusing ; but amidst all these accomplishments the one
thing needful is that it should not forget to be itself. And
that is what, in Spenser's hands, it never forgets. He is
a learned poet and a wise man ; but though his poetry is
often as edifying as a sermon, and often as full of wonders
as a fairy tale, it is always poetry first and fairy tale or
sermon only second and so far as poetry allows. Dwarf or
giant, mystery or morality, arts or arms, Greek myth or

---

[1] *Poems of Spenser.* Selected and with an Introduction by W. B.
Yeats. The Golden Poets. Jack.

Christian doctrine, it is all the same; whatever Spenser touches becomes pure gold of poetry. His very faults are such as could belong only to a poet. When he is dull, it is not, like Wordsworth, because he thinks he is in the pulpit, but because, like Shelley, he forgets he is on the earth. Or rather, while he lets Memory, mother of the Muses, and Imagination, their eldest daughter, carry him away captive into strange countries, and delights his fancy in weaving story within story and adding episode to episode, he forgets that poetry, if it is to be a fine art, must dwell in Cosmos and not in Chaos, that order and limit are necessary parts of the constitution of the human mind, that the most poetic sort of confusion is still confusion and not creation, and that the end of confusion is weariness and sleep. Still, these are faults that the rest of the world may envy. Just as we are not ethereal enough to live long with Shelley, we are not mobile enough, we have not enough of music in us, to keep mind and ear long travelling with Spenser. We sink back in exhausted surrender. But there is consolation even so. Of all places of poetic slumber, the softest are to be found among the stanzas of the *Faery Queen*.

Besides the poems, this little volume contains some coloured illustrations by Miss Jessie King, a glossary of archaic words, some notes, and an Introduction by Mr. W. B. Yeats. The illustrations are pretty enough, but of no special importance. The glossary might almost as well have been omitted. People who want one at all want something very different from this. A glossary which contains only about seventy words, and does not include such rare words as 'say' ('his garment neither was of silk nor say'), 'herye,' 'dernly,' 'underfong,' or many others that might be cited, is little better than an imposture. Nor can notes which carefully tell us who the sons of Leda were, and who Alcides was, while they entirely ignore many of the real difficulties, be said to be of much greater value. The Introduction is, of course, a different matter. Mr. Yeats is not only a poet himself; he is one of our very few original thinkers about poetry. His *Ideas of Good and Evil* is perhaps the most suggestive and the most stimulating piece of literary criticism that has appeared in England in recent years. But of course he has the defects of his qualities. The worst of original ideas is that their possessors are so apt to fancy that they cover the whole ground. The joy and pride of a new thought are such that they make it appear the key to all knowledge.

It has been Mr. Yeats's mission, admirably discharged both in his verse and in his prose, to remind us of an element in poetry too easily forgotten in a critical and self-conscious age, the element of spontaneous mysticism resulting in what Matthew Arnold called 'natural magic'. And he has carried still further Arnold's striking suggestion that this element in English poetry belongs to the Celtic strain in us. He points us back to the half-lost fountain-head of poetry, the 'troubled ecstasy' in the presence of nature which is the most ancient religion of the world. So far we may all go with him. We can all see that Teutonic intellectualism and Teutonic seriousness have had at least their full share of influence over us during the last three centuries. But when these yearnings after the beautiful infancy of art pass into a denunciation of all ordered action and all ordered thought, when we are assured that Shakespeare must have preferred Richard II to Henry V, and that Henry V is only the supreme instance of the law 'that the commonplace shall inherit the earth', then we begin to wish for Matthew Arnold back again, and a little more judgement to control the overflowing exuberance of an original idea. He, at least, would not have told us that Henry V was a smaller man than Richard II 'in the Divine Hierarchies'. He could love and praise the Celtic side of us, but he knew the other side— and, one may add, the facts—too well to run into such a grotesque absurdity as the statement made by Mr. Yeats in this Introduction that, if one of the poets who threw their verses into Sidney's grave were to come to life again to-day, 'he would find some shadow of the life he knew, though not the art he knew, among young men in Paris, and would think that his true country'. There have been losses in England since Sidney's day, no doubt, but England then, as now, was England and not France. Let us go back, if we can, to the fine sensitiveness of our childhood when there was 'no man mowing in a meadow' who did not see visions, as is still the case in Ireland, according to Mr. Yeats ; let us keep all we may of the 'high instincts' that startle our dullness out of its complacent routine, and the 'blank misgivings' that come to tell us the primary truth of all poetry and all religion, that the idea is greater than the fact, the spirit than the letter, and the only things supremely worth knowing those that never have been or will be proved. The more we can do that the better. But the wise man who wishes back the innocence of his childhood would not, if he could, divest himself of the wisdom of his riper years. There is a time for all things. The beautiful childishness of children is no ornament to age. And it is a kind of childishness to wish to forget all we have learned in 300 years, to wish to keep the intellect out of poetry, to see the weakness of Puritanism so plainly as to be unable to see its strength, to think of the learning of the Renaissance, the moral earnestness of the seventeenth century, the intelligence of the eighteenth, and the practical energy of the nineteenth, as all alike enemies to the poetic spirit. This is not only blind and narrow; it is a treachery to the all-embracing empire of poetry. We cannot if we would be Celtic tribesmen again, and we would not if we could be Irish peasants. It is not for nothing that we have known the beautiful art of Spenser, the noble seriousness of Milton, the profound wisdom of Wordsworth. We shall not wish with Mr. Yeats that

Spenser had renounced his Renaissance birthright to model himself exclusively upon Malory and the Minstrels; still less shall we be in danger of so amazing a delusion as that which sees in him a poet 'who gave his heart to the State', who 'had no deep moral or religious life', and whose 'morality is official and impersonal'. One would have expected something saner from so fine a poet and critic as Mr. Yeats. But these are the strange places a man gets into when he judges English poets by Irish political prejudice, and, measuring poetry by the measure of a single idea, narrows down her wide world-embracing kingdom to the hills and pastures where it began.

Spenser knew better. He was too wise to deny himself the great possibilities opened out to him by the new learning. He could look back wistfully on the heroic side of feudalism, and keep it alive, so far as might be, in his great poem; he could cling longingly to the old language that was passing away; but the old ignorance, the old rude and barbarous incoherence, the old childishness, had no friend in him. He rejoiced through all his being in the ordered splendours of the new art. In his delighted hands they attained at once to all but their highest height. And though Milton's art is greater than his, it is still true that for pure loveliness, for enchanting and bewitching beauty, Spenser is without a rival. He loves to let the senses lie still in the garden of the world, the eye wandering round among its pictured splendours, the ear drinking in its multitude of delicious sounds; and who has succeeded in getting so much of their essence into poetry as he? To other poets other excellences; but this belongs to Spenser. The whole deliciousness of the earth is in his poetry; when she makes her bed smoothest, when her outline is softest, it is not softer or smoother than the rise and fall of his verse. Everything is to be found in it, as in his own 'Island of Love'.

No tree, that is of count, in greenewood growes,
From lowest juniper to ceder tall,
No flowre in field, that daintie odour throwes,
And deckes his branch with blossomes over all,
But there was planted, or grew naturall:
Nor sense of man so coy and curious nice,
But there mote find to please itself withal:
Nor hart could wish for any quaint device
But there it present was, and did fraile sense entice.

    .   .   .   .

Fresh shadowes, fit to shroud from sunny ray;
Faire lawnds, to take the sunne in season dew;
Sweet springs, in which a thousand Nymphes did play;
Soft rombling brookes, that gentle slomber drew;
High reared mounts, the lands about to vew;
Low looking dales disloignd from common gaze;
Delightful bowres, to solace lovers trew;
False Labyrinthes, fond runners eyes to daze;
All which by nature made did nature selfe amaze.

All the men of the Renaissance were occupied in looking at the beauty of the world to which mediaeval asceticism had for so many centuries tried to blind all human eyes; and no one looked more lovingly than Spenser, or saw things lovelier. But in all ages the first result of this delicious surrender to the charm of the world is the bitter realization of its brief and fragile life. The Spenser of the nineteenth century found it so; no world was ever fairer than his; but it was a world—

Where youth grows pale and spectre-thin and dies;
  Where but to think is to be full of sorrow
    And leaden-eyed despairs;
Where Beauty cannot keep her lustrous eyes,
  Or new Love pine at them beyond to-morrow.

There is the nemesis of all sensuousness, even the most beautiful and the most innocent. And as it sweeps most mercilessly on young poets, so it has never fallen harder than it fell on the men of the Renaissance when all the world of letters was young. We see it everywhere, across the Channel in Ronsard and in Du Bellay; the pure soul

of Sidney is touched by it as well as the vast ambition of
Raleigh, and the supreme genius of Shakespeare. But
there is no one out of whom it struck more beautiful music
than Spenser. Over and over again in his poetry there is
some one to

> chaunt this lovely lay :
> Ah! see, whoso fayre thing doest faine to see,
> In springing flowre the image of thy day.
> Ah! see the Virgin Rose, how sweetly shee
> Doth first peepe foorth with bashfull modestee,
> That fairer seemes the lesse ye see her may.
> Lo! see soone after how more bold and free
> Her bared bosome she doth broade display ;
> Lo! see soone after how she fades and falls away.
>
> So passeth, in the passing of a day,
> Of mortall life the leafe, the bud, the flowre ;
> Ne more doth florish after first decay,
> That earst was sought to deck both bed and bowre
> Of many a lady, and many a Paramowre.
> Gather therefore the Rose whilest yet is prime,
> For soone comes age that will her pride deflowre ;
> Gather the Rose of love whilest yet is time,
> Whilest loving thou mayst loved be with equall crime.

Mr. Yeats does full justice to this side of Spenser's genius ;
and he well recognizes that it goes beyond a mere physical
sensuousness. As he says, Spenser 'began in English poetry,
despite a temperament that delighted in sensuous beauty
alone with perfect delight, that worship of Intellectual
Beauty which Shelley carried to a much greater subtlety
and applied to the whole of life'. The strange thing is that
seeing so much he sees no more. How is it that so fine
a critic has let Irish prejudice against Spenser's politics and
religion blind him to the pure vein of spiritual ecstasy that
runs all through the poet's genius ? The author of the great
Hymns, the creator of Una, had, according to Mr. Yeats,
'no deep moral or religious life.' Such things as his 'pro-
cessions of deadly sins' are 'an unconscious hypocrisy'. No
one would pretend that Spenser's faith is like Dante's, or

his moral earnestness like Milton's ; but no man whose attitude towards these things was 'official and impersonal' could have found for it such utterance as he finds, not once, but again and again :—

> None thereof worthy be, but those whom shee
> Vouchsafeth to her presence to receave,
> And letteth them her lovely face to see,
> Whereof such wondrous pleasures they conceave,
> And sweete contentment, that it doth bereave
> Their soul of sense, through infinite delight
> And them transport from flesh into the spright.

It is, one must suppose, this curious blindness to Spenser's spiritual side that has caused Mr. Yeats, while including and warmly praising the two fine cantos called 'Mutabilitie' with which the *Faery Queen*, as we have it, closes, to omit the two final stanzas which Dean Church chose to be the last word of his book on Spenser. Yet it can hardly be altogether an accident that the poet paused in his great work with such a stanza as this :—

> Then gin I thinke on that which Nature sayd,
> Of that same time when no more Change shall be
> But steadfast rest of all things, firmely stayd
> Upon the pillours of Eternity
> That is contrayr to Mutabilitie ;
> For all that moveth doth in Change delight :
> But thenceforth all shall rest eternally
> With Him that is the God of Sabaoth hight :
> O! that great Sabaoth God, grant me that Sabaoth's sight !

The whole poem is a foretaste of Milton, as Mr. Yeats himself confesses ; but nothing in it is so Miltonic as this noble stanza, in which we begin to hear the sublime note of the opening of *Comus*, of the final vision of *Lycidas*, of 'Blest Pair of Sirens'.

That is the whole truth about Spenser. He is the poet of some of the loveliest things in English verse, the poet whose

> delitious harmony
> In full straunge notes was sweetly heard to sound
> That the rare sweetness of the melody
> The feeble senses wholly did confound,
> And the frayle soule in deepe delight nigh drownd.

He is the poet of such astonishing lines as—

> Nought is there under heaven's wide hollowness,

and

> This is the port of rest from troublous toyle
> The worldes sweet Inn from paine and wearisome
>   turmoyle,

and

>   careless Quiet lies
> Wrapt in eternal silence farre from enemies,

and

> By this the northerne waggoner had set
> His sevenfold teeme behind the steadfast starre
> That was in oceans waves yet never wet ;
> But firme is fixt, and sendeth light from farre
> To all that in the wide deep wandering are,

and, loveliest of all, perhaps, of

> Sleepe after toyle, port after stormie seas,
> Ease after warre, death after life, does greatly please.

He is all this ; but he is more too. The 'perfect ease of
that sweet weariness' of the senses has, indeed, never
found such expression as he gave it ; but he is more than
the poet of any mere sensuous passiveness, however exquisitely spoken. No one has ever read the *Faery Queen*
without feeling that it was a school of honour as well as
a paradise of beautiful things and a forest of strange adventures. No one reads it without being certain that its poet
was no mere languid dreamer of the dreams of the senses.
In spite of all the strength he lavished on the bower of
Acrasia, his poem as a whole remains a trumpet-call to the
praise of brave men and the honour of pure women. We
feel that the real man is in it. Indeed, the moralist is so
real and strong that he sometimes forces himself upon the

poet at the expense of dramatic probability, as may be seen
in the discourse of Despair to the Red Cross Knight, much
of which is so little like the language of a fiend that it
might very well be used by a saint at the deathbed of a
penitent. But even that is not all. Spenser is, in his
measure, a poet of the great vision. More than any man
in that day, he knew how to show the way for Milton to
mount up to those soaring heights of rapture in which
music and splendour mingle in a glory of celestial light.
'Blest Pair of Sirens' is, indeed, a flight beyond his reach;
but none of his contemporaries could approach so near it as
the poet who called upon Love to lift him

> Farre above reach of feeble earthly sight,

and began his 'heavenly hymn' with such a stanza as
this:—

> Before this world's great frame in which all things
> Are now containd found any being-place,
> Ere flitting Time could wag his eyas wings
> About that mightie bound which doth embrace
> The rolling Spheres, and parts their hours by space,
> That High Eternall Powre, which now doth move
> In all these things, moved in it selfe by love.

Spenser was not, it is true, a religious poet in the narrower
sense, a poet of the order of Campion, or Crashaw, or Francis
Thompson. But assuredly such language as that of this
stanza, or the last lines of 'Mutabilitie', would not have
risen easily to the lips of a man of 'no deep moral or
religious life'. No mere poet of the senses or the intellect,
no alien to the world of spirit, could have found or even
borrowed it. And the fact that it came to Spenser is proof
that he was neither.

SHAKESPEARE'S TRAGEDIES [1]

THE world is, by this time, a little weary of being lectured. Hardly Coleridge himself, uniting the attractions of poet and high-priest, hardly Carlyle, the 'mad labourer' with the voice of a Hebrew prophet, could to-day make a fashionable sensation by the announcement of a course of lectures. Still less is a busy metropolitan world, even that section of it which cares at all for literature, apt often to have ears for any rumour of fame taking its origin in the class-room of a University professor. But Mr. Bradley had hardly begun his lectures before the echo of his voice made itself heard beyond the academic boundaries. Occupant of a chair that has more often than any other in Oxford claimed and received the attention of all that is intelligent in the English-speaking world, he at once showed that his tenure of it was to be among the most distinguished in its history. It was known that the lectures he was giving on Shakespeare were making a very unusual impression in Oxford, and those who had not the chance of hearing them looked forward with eagerness to their publication. That is now accomplished in the volume before us, on which there can be only one verdict. The book is a great achievement. Nothing has been written for many years that has done so much as these lectures will do to advance the understanding and appreciation of the greatest things in Shakespeare's greatest plays. One may go further, indeed, without going too far. It is not merely a question of Shakespearean studies. One may well doubt whether in the whole field of English literary criticism anything has

[1] *Shakespearean Tragedy.* Lectures on *Hamlet, Othello, King Lear, Macbeth.* By A. C. Bradley, Professor of Poetry in the University of Oxford. Macmillan.

been written in the last twenty years more luminous, more masterly, more penetrating to the very centre of its subject. The task before a man who writes a study of a great poet may be said to be to make it a certainty that no intelligent person who will read both the poet's text and the critic's interpretation can fail to get at the root of the matter. It is not so often accomplished as might be supposed. Matthew Arnold did it, as it were by accident, for Homer, while affecting to talk only of Homeric translation. Mr. Raleigh more recently has done it for Wordsworth. A man who has read Homer or Wordsworth, and still misses the point about him after reading Arnold or Mr. Raleigh will never find it. Did not Johnson once break out, 'Sir, I can find you arguments, but I am not bound to find you understanding'? And so with this book. If there is any one who, after reading the four tragedies and what Mr. Bradley has to say about them, is still in the dark as to the essential lines of Shakespeare's achievement as a tragic poet, he will never come into the light.

Shakespeare is a large subject, and not a little of Mr. Bradley's wisdom is seen in the part of it he has chosen to deal with. Books may be written about Shakespeare's language, about his versification, about his relation to his contemporaries, about his debt to his sources, and fifty similar subjects, and they all have their use and their interest. But their interest is secondary, because they leave untouched the central and primary question which we desire to have answered about him. So, again, other books may be written about his life, his family, his private affairs, his success in business; and they too are well enough in their way. But, for the essential issue, for the key to Shakespeare as the master mind, they are irrelevant, and almost impertinent. The attention cannot be concentrated on them without grave dangers. Occupy yourself, as Mr. Sidney Lee has done, too exclusively with Shakespeare's business achievements, and you come to quote with approval Pope's

> For gain, not glory, winged his roving flight
> And grew immortal in his own despite,

and to inform us that Shakespeare 'chiefly valued his literary attainments and successes as serving the prosaic end of providing permanently for himself and his daughters'. Mr. Bradley has had his face turned in another direction, so that he has escaped these dangers. So far as we can remember, neither the Globe Theatre, nor the town of Stratford, nor New Place is so much as once mentioned in his book. Thus when he alludes to Pope's lines it is in quite a different tone. He is saying that Shakespeare was evidently sometimes weary and indifferent, and thought the whole affair of play-writing a little thing. But, he adds, 'none of these thoughts and feelings influenced him when his subject had caught hold of him. To imagine that *then* he " winged his roving flight " for "gain" or "glory", or wrote from any cause on earth but the necessity of expression, with all its pains and raptures, is mere folly.' There is the advantage of having the eye fixed on the centre of the subject. Great as Shakespeare is in so many ways he is greatest of all as a tragedian; and the greatest of his tragedies are unquestionably *Lear*, *Hamlet*, *Othello*, and *Macbeth*. In devoting himself, there-fore, first to a study of Shakespeare's general aim and method as a tragedian, and then to a detailed examination of these four plays, Mr. Bradley keeps his finger on the very heart of the poet, and deals with that part of his achievement which is of all the most essential, the most universal, the most immortal.

The fascination of the highest literature lies in part in its being a thing of infinite reach, stretching out towards far things in heaven and hell which it can never wholly grasp. It always suggests much that it can never say. There the fragments lie, all that Shakespeare could tell us, perhaps, and we must read them as we can, every man for himself. 'We are all seekers still,' as Matthew Arnold said ; that is the eternal fascination of literature as of life. Hence, in the case of a book like this, an almost unbounded admiration is far from implying invariable agreement with Mr. Bradley's views. For instance, his attempt to set aside the Schlegel-Coleridge explanation of Hamlet's inaction as caused by an over-reflective habit and to substitute for it an access of melancholia caused by his mother's marriage does not appear to us very convincing. Indeed, for the most part, it seems to be hardly more than a refinement of the other. The passages alleged to disprove Coleridge's view, such as the transition at the end of Act I from the desire of vengeance to the wish, not as Mr. Bradley says never to have been born, but never to have been born to set the world right, or that other transition from ' O ! what a rogue and peasant slave am I ' to doubts as whether the ghost was a devil, seem to us just as explicable by the reflective habit, which sees all difficulties and listens to all doubts, as by Mr. Bradley's theory of a special melancholy. And again, in his masterly study of the characters of Macbeth and Lady Macbeth he hardly appears to bring out the essential point. No previous critic, perhaps, has so clearly shown that the chief difference between the two is that Macbeth is a highly imaginative character and Lady Macbeth the very reverse. And he is the first, so far as we remember, to insist so fully on the point that Lady Macbeth's steady decline in mind and body after the murder is due to the fact that owing to her lack of imagination she had gone into it without any conception of what its dread consciousness would be. But he does not take the final step which seems to us to set the crown on Shakespeare's wonderful delineation of the two characters. Macbeth, the imaginative man, has gone through all the horrors that the

murder will bring with it before ever he can bring himself
to do the deed. His awful experience is before, not after,
the murder, and, like all men of imagination, when once
embarked on a course of which he has experienced all the
difficulties by anticipation, nothing daunts him. He
hesitates at nothing, acts swiftly and ruthlessly, and at the
very end can say 'I have almost forgot the taste of fears',
and go to his death with unbroken vigour of body and mind.
Then, again, though Mr. Bradley is not afraid of confessing
Shakespeare's weaknesses, so loyal a Shakespearian might
well have gone further without danger of being misunderstood. Can any explanation, for instance, even one so
ingenious as Mr. Bradley's, alter the fact that every one
feels Cordelia's conduct in the first scene of *King Lear* not
only harsh and disagreeable, but the most unconvincing
thing in any serious work of Shakespeare? It is not that
we are surprised when it occurs; in good literature we are
always being surprised by things when they occur; but
it is that the surprise remains as we look back on it, and
never diminishes as the right surprises of literature do.
Strangeness is no defect in art, as Mr. Bradley points out
elsewhere; what is a defect, as he adds, is anything out of
character. And will any one ever persuade himself that
it is natural or dramatically probable that a daughter so
loving and so loved as Cordelia would treat her aged father
in that hard, rigid, obstinate fashion?

Many other points of difference with Mr. Bradley, of
smaller or greater importance, might be made, but neither
space nor inclination encourages discussion of them. Only
in general we would say that he is at his best in the large
questions and at his weakest in the details. He is apt to
consider words too curiously and find too much in them.
It is surely quite fanciful, for instance, to see any democratic sympathies in Hamlet's 'He was a *man* take him for
all in all', or to see an allusion to his father's death in his

signing himself, as all Elizabethan lovers did, 'the most unhappy Prince Hamlet.' And Mr. Bradley falls sometimes into
the weakness of wanting to make all Shakespeare's details
fit into each other as if they were pieces of a puzzle. It is a
vain occupation. The inconsistencies of time which we can
all discover if we choose in each of the four tragedies when
we read them, and never notice when we see them on the
stage, are enough, even if they stood alone, to show that
Shakespeare was either unconscious of them altogether, or
knew of them and did not care because no playgoer would
care either, nor indeed any reader who reads to enjoy and
not to ask questions. But these are among the small things
of the book; and even of them the far larger number open
our eyes to new points of interest or beauty. And when we
turn to the great things, too great to be dwelt on here, the
criticism responds as adequately as criticism can to the
tremendous demands made on it by the poet. It is impossible to say more. What is the ultimate impression left by
these mighty pictures of human fate? What forces ultimately control us? In whose hands, our own, the hands of
God, or the hands of chance, do our destinies lie? Is it
a power of good, or a power of evil, or a blind fate, that is
behind the veil? Shakespeare never plainly answers such
questions, though such a man must have thought about
them. Perhaps the answer he found was too uncertain,
perhaps it was too great to find fit audience at the Globe
Theatre. But tragedy cannot but bring its poet face to face
with these problems; and even though Shakespeare found
it impossible, either because it would have been undramatic,
or for deeper reasons, to set out any explaining creed or
philosophy of life, the tragedian who shows us a human
shambles as, in one sense, the only solution found by the
troubled world of Hamlet or Lear knows that we must ask
how and why that should be so. And, as he describes such
scenes, he cannot altogether avoid giving some hint by the

words he uses, by the mere tone of his voice, of the way in which he read the mystery. Two painters paint a Crucifixion; and we know at once for which of them it is an event in Jewish history, and for which it is the event on which the world hangs. And so we may, and must, question Shakespeare as we question Aeschylus and Sophocles. We are right to wish to know what such men thought of such problems. And what is the answer we get? Not a plain answer, certainly. Imagination, whether we look at in Michael Angelo or in Blake or in the Book of Job, always feels that such questions belong to a world high above the exact definitions in which science vainly fancies all truth can be stated. No Church or sect or philosophical school can claim Shakespeare as her own. Even to attempt to put into prose the impression left by the tragedies, as Mr. Bradley does, though right and inevitable, ought only to be done, as he does it, with a consciousness that one is measuring the heavens and translating the voice of the winds. Then, setting that confession of humility on our foreheads, and bearing in mind that prose can never utter more than a tiny fragment of the message of poetry, we may read all Mr. Bradley says and conclude that the answer of the tragedies to such questions is neither the Christian answer of Divine providence, guidance, and judgement, nor the Lucretian answer of Divine indifference, but a mystery that lies between them; though it is not the less moving and even strengthening for being a mystery.

But we may, perhaps, go further than Mr. Bradley. For when we see that at the end of all the tragedies, mighty as is the havoc wrought by the principle of death, yet what is ultimately left standing is 'a family or a city or a country' which, however exhausted, is 'alive through the principle of good which animates it', and with it 'individuals who have won our respect and confidence', we may be inclined to conclude that of the two sides of the mystery Shakespeare definitely leans to that which suggests that 'existence in an order ultimately depends on good, and that if the presence of evil is hostile to such existence, the inner being, or soul, of this order must be of one nature with good'. And, indeed, is not this after all a very slight extension of what Mr. Bradley so finely describes as the ultimate impression the great tragedies leave on us? We see Hamlet fail, and Lear and Cordelia die, and Othello murder Desdemona. And as we watch we do not ask for a philosophic justification of things happening so. For we are left with an 'impression that the heroic being, though in one sense and outwardly he has failed, is yet in another sense superior to the world in which he appears; is, in some way, which we do not seek to define, untouched by the doom which overtakes him; and is rather set free from life than deprived of it'. And this impression really 'implies an idea which, if developed, would transform the tragic view of things'. For it implies that the tragic world, if taken as it is presented, with all its error, guilt, failures, woe, and waste, is no final reality, but only a part of reality taken for the whole, and, when so taken, illusive; and that if we could see the whole, and the tragic facts in their true place in it, we should find them, not abolished, of course, but so transmuted that they had ceased to be strictly tragic—find, perhaps, the suffering and death counting for little or nothing, the greatness of the soul for much or all, and the heroic spirit, in spite of failure, nearer to the heart of things than the smaller, more circumspect, and perhaps even 'better' beings who survive the catastrophe.

Has any one ever put better into words the little that can be put of our feelings as the curtain falls over the dead Hamlet, or we turn the last page of Othello? And is it an intrusion on the reserve of Shakespeare to say that the poet who gave us feelings of this sort as the last he wished us to carry away from him must have had also, in some fashion, we may not say what, his share of a 'faith that looks through death', a faith which finds death of little account because it 'sees into the life of things'?

MOLIÈRE[1]

THE plays of Molière are the pleasure-ground of all the world. No fame is securer than his, and only one or two more universal. So long as our civilization remains, Molière remains. So long as human beings enjoy the spectacle of human life, so long as they retain that distinguishing mark of civilization as opposed to barbarism, the capacity to be intellectually amused, they can never forget Molière. So much we may say for the whole world of men and women who are so far civilized, at any rate, as to have added social and intellectual pleasures to those of the senses and the passions. And for the elect whose civilization has gone a stage further, so that they find one of their keenest pleasures in the mere sight of a piece of work perfectly done, Molière is all that he is for the rest, and this besides. The particular thing that he set out to do is done, impeccably, unalterably, finally, so that just those who have most skill in such matters are the most certain that a thousand years of labour could not do it better. There it is, done once for all, like a few big things in the world's history and a few small, like the *Aeneid* of Virgil, like the immortal trifles of Catullus, like Milton, like Jane Austen. The world outside France has remained rather cold in the presence of some of those whom France acclaims as her highest, but about the universal homage to Molière there has never been any serious doubt. Now and then, especially at first, a pedant with a half-understood Aristotle under his arm has

[1] *The Plays of Molière in French.* With an English Translation and Notes by A. R. Waller, M.A., and an Introduction by George Saintsbury. Eight volumes. Edinburgh : John Grant.

tried to persuade the worshippers that they had come to a false oracle which did not speak according to the rules. But the crowd knows what it comes for and whether it goes away empty. *Securus iudicat orbis terrarum.* The house of Molière will always be full and happy ; and, if any rule of art be cited against the legitimacy of the happiness, those who are tasting it will always dismiss the intrusive objector with their poet's own question : 'Je voudrais bien savoir si la grande règle de toutes les règles n'est pas de plaire.' After all, that is the test from which there is no appeal. The business of art is to please, and, with only one qualification, that old and important one, 'semper, omnibus, ubique,' it is safe to add that the art which pleases is good art. But Molière's fame has no fear of those three great words. Their sound has indeed usually been heard in a world that lies out of his reach, but, in their plain and literal sense, there have been very few things to which they can be so truthfully applied as they can to him and to the universal popularity of his comedy. Neither *Tartuffe* and *Le Misanthrope* nor *Scapin* and *Le Bourgeois Gentilhomme* were the kind of thing that attracts crowds for two months and is unreadable in two years. Their author was popular in his lifetime, and he has been popular ever since. He is the glory of France and the delight of all the world. To-day, as in his own day, people who read or see a play of his for the first time are constantly paying him La Fontaine's instantaneous tribute, 'Voilà mon homme !' There are many things he is not. But that he is, and will be so long as our civilization lasts ; the man whom everybody likes at once, and never stops liking.

No stronger evidence of his position in England could well be given than the appearance of the present edition. Is there any other French author, any other foreign author at all, with the single exception of Dante, who could be issued in this way, in eight volumes, with the original text on one side and an English translation facing it? These elaborate methods have generally been reserved for the great Greeks and Latins. But here is Molière, done in the same way for all the English world; with the French text for those who need no other, the English version for those who know no French, and the two together for the many who prefer travelling on the original road, but need a little help over a stile now and then. Altogether, the book ought to be the giver of a good many happy evenings this winter, and for many winters and summers to come. The only pity is that it is impossible to give unreserved praise to the translation. One hates to seem ungrateful to any one who, like Mr. Waller, has performed a long and arduous service to the republic of letters (such as that of making a complete translation of Molière undoubtedly is), but the truth is the truth, and it compels one to say that his rendering is passable rather than ideal. He decided, after indulging for a moment the ludicrous fancy of Molière in English blank verse, that not even rhymed couplets, but plain prose was the proper English dress for Molière to wear; and that was plainly the right decision. But unluckily his prose gives us far less than might be given of the peculiar manner of Molière. Of course, one does not want it to call up French idioms, and, to do it justice, it has very little of that worst fault of the translator; but one does want it to call up Molière, and that is what it, to a great extent, fails to do. The right rule is, all the peculiarities that belong to the author, none that belong merely to his language; and the best example of it is Jowett's Plato, where not one ounce of Plato is lost and not one ounce of Greek retained. Translators, like other authors, may reasonably shrink from the severe compliment of being tried by the highest standard. But it is fair, as well as desirable, for the critic to keep it in view, provided he does not demand that it should be always and exactly attained. It is not easy, no

doubt, to be as full of life and point in English as Molière
is in French; but it ought to be easy to get nearer than
such a sentence as 'I should be a fool indeed to interfere;
I might get hurt', out of which half the life of the *Bourgeois
Gentilhomme's* 'je serais bien fou de m'aller fourrer parmi
eux pour recevoir quelque coup qui me ferait mal' seems
somehow to have evaporated. So, again, in the same play,
'N'irez-vous point l'un de ces jours au collége vous faire
donner le fouet à votre âge' loses more of its savour than
need be lost in 'Will you not go to school, one of these
days, and be birched? It would be a nice thing at your
age.' Surely half the point lies in ' vous faire donner'; with
its suggestion of ' get them to give you the birch', which
Mr. Waller loses altogether. Or, once more, does not 'I don't
believe I am wrong in thinking him hard hit' give an un-
necessarily faint image of the verve of the original, with its
pointed repetition, 'je pense qu'il en tient, et je crois penser
bien'? Are we not entitled to ask for something more
vivid, more sparkling, more arresting than this, in a word,
something more Molieresque? Nor is the translation always
impeccable in the matter of correctness. To take a few
examples from a single play, *L'École des Femmes*, the word
'valet' in English is not the equivalent of the French
'valet', a much more inclusive word; and the 'sociétés
déréglées', which are said, in the eighth of Arnolphe's
maxims for wives, to corrupt the minds of women, are not
'rowdy meetings', as Mr. Waller renders them, but rather
'dissolute' or 'loose' gatherings. The point is not their
noise, but their morals. So again, to translate ' Mais d'un
trop pur amour mon âme est embrasée' by ' but my love for
her is twined round with too honourable bonds for that' is
simply a blunder, and rather a bad one; and much the
same is true of 'Do you believe I have anything to be
proud of in that, or, indeed, that I do not know quite well
that I am a stupid?' as a rendering of:—

Croit-on que je me flatte, et qu'enfin, dans ma tête,
Je ne juge pas bien que je suis une bête ?

There are too many of these mistakes. On the other
hand, it is only fair to say that there are some things in
the translation which could hardly be bettered, such as,
for instance, the difficult scene in dialect between Charlotte
and Pierrot in *Don Juan*, of which Mr. Waller gives a very
spirited and humorous version in something like the language of Tennyson's 'Northern Farmer'; keeping to his
dialect, it may be added, with much more strict verisimili-
tude than Molière keeps to his. On the whole, it may be
said that the translation is a useful piece of work which
those who do not expect too much will be glad to have on
their shelves. Nobody must hope to receive from it more
than the scantiest fragment of that continuous literary and
intellectual luxury which the judicious enjoy in Molière's
French; but people who like an English companion to go
through the plays with them, and are content to forgo the
fine flowers of literary sensation, will find their account in
it reasonably well.

The translation is preceded by an introduction by Mr.
George Saintsbury, which is what everybody will expect it
to be. There is, of course, the usual irritating style as of
an everlasting talker who is determined no one else shall
get a word in, and so plays himself the part of his own
listener or critic, anticipating all comments or objections
in an unending series of parentheses. There is the usual
superabundance of unnecessary allusions and quotations,
the usual scraps of French, and the usual clumsy phrases
of the type of 'the old half-destroyed and soon-to-be-
destroyed-utterly palace of the unlucky Constable'. And
of course there is the usual wide and genuine knowledge
of the subject. The introduction is mainly occupied with
a chronological account of Molière's life and writings, and
a discussion of the theatre as it existed in his day; but

there are some final pages devoted to a critical estimate. It contains at least one sentence which every critic worth his salt will want to quote and wish to have said himself. Mr. Saintsbury has been saying that he finds the essence of Molière neither in style and form, nor in craftsmanship, nor even in the Shakesperean power of investing everything with life, but in the habit of regarding all the world as so much material which is to be taken or rejected according as laughter can or cannot be made out of it. Molière is in fact 'the Master of the Laugh'. No doubt he sees the tears and shame of the world as well. But they are not his affair. 'To obtrude the pity, or the shame, or the sin, or the moral of any kind was not his object or his business. The object and the business were to isolate the *ludicrum saeculi*—to put "the way of the world" in a comic light of eternity.' There is Molière. The way of his plays is the way of the world, and the light he sometimes streams and sometimes flashes upon it is the light of comedy, held in the hand of the Master of the Laugh : and yet it is also the light of eternity, the only light in which great art can see to do its work, the light which shows the whole, which is well aware in its laughter that laughter is not all, and looks through its tears to an ultimate solution in which tears are transcended.

But, illuminating as that saying of Mr. Saintsbury's is, it cannot cover the whole ground. Like so many critical *dicta*, in answering one question it raises another. It gives us the essence of comedy in an admirable phrase ; but the essence of Molière, the thing which distinguishes him from other comedians, does it give that equally clearly ? It is impossible not to ask oneself why the taste left on the intellectual palate by *Tartuffe* or *Le Misanthrope* is so different from that left by, say, *Henry IV*. Part of the explanation lies, no doubt, in the fact that Molière was of Latin stock, with the Latin turn for order, definiteness, lucidity, while in Shakespeare, as in most Teutons, there are not infrequent traces of the primordial chaos of the human mind. But that is not all; for there is Rabelais, who is an unhewn mass of originality, learning, reforming ardour, and obscenity, and Rabelais was a Frenchman. Part again lies in the different social stage of the two poets. France was fifty years ahead of England in these matters, and Molière was fifty years younger than Shakespeare, so that his world shows a century of social advance, for good or for evil, upon Shakespeare's. It is a far more coherent organized world; indeed, it is close upon that fatal stage—where, however, as Jane Austen shows, comedy can still enjoy herself—in which society has taken the place of humanity. When we put ourselves in Molière's hands, we must not hope to get away any more into Shakespeare's fields and forests; our poet had done more travelling than he cared for by the time he got to Paris, and he will not again quit the Court and the parlour, except now and then for the back stairs. And so he has no room for the Shakespearean, Falstaffian, laugh, 'broad as ten thousand beeves at pasture,' as Mr. Meredith says. That is a thing of the hillside, not of four walls rather crowded with polite persons. But it is astonishing to see what he can do within these limits, and how he can make these polite persons rise above the reserves and restrictions of politeness. The action of *Tartuffe*, after all, takes place in the drawing-room.

But, if Molière knows how to carry people away with him, it is not by poetry that he does it. Indeed, he is scarcely at all a poet, and his great creations never make the poetic escapes from the world of every day that sooner or later come to nearly all Shakespeare's. He is simply a man of incomparable lucidity, of sovereign sanity, who worked on life by the means of comedy. His theatre cannot be compared with that of Shakespeare. It is an altogether smaller and quieter thing. Its well-ordered comedy has no

chance of giving us the shuddering intensity of pleasure
and pain which we experience as we watch Shakespeare
walking his tight-rope of genius with the gulf of bathos
on the one side, and the gulf of madness on the other,
and so often walking it without a fall. The pleasure of
Molière is quite different from that—the sort of pleasure
that can be taken in perfect ease in the stall at the theatre,
in the armchair by the fire. But what an exquisite pleasure
it is! What quality and distinction it has! What a delightful play of the mind is set going by it! After all, one
comes back to that; it is the proper pleasure of a civilized
being. Molière's laugh may not be as big, as broadly
human, as Shakespeare's; but no laugh in the world was
ever so finely planned, so exquisitely carried out. If Shakespeare always makes him seem rather small, he can in
return sometimes make Shakespeare seem clumsy. He is
the master of his laugh, not his laugh of him, as is sometimes the case with Shakespeare, and often with Rabelais.
Only once, perhaps, does it run away with him—in those
last scenes of *Le Bourgeois Gentilhomme*—just as only once
in all his life did his impeccable sanity of judgement forget
itself enough to let him choose an impossible subject to
work upon. Even then he handles it so brilliantly that
critics have been found to call *Don Juan* his masterpiece.
But such utterances show more loyalty than judgement.
There is no dancing on a volcano, and no jesting in hell;
the story, too horrible even for tragedy, is utterly impossible
for comedy; and, in spite of its good things, the play is,
what it was doomed from the first to be, an ambitious
failure. But it is its author's one aberration. Everywhere
else his good sense is as omnipresent as his comic power,
and our enjoyment of the follies of humanity, as they are
shown to us in his theatre, would not be nearly so un-
alloyed, if our belief in our own kind were not sustained all
the while by the incomparable good sense of the showman.

Homo sum, we feel with his great predecessor: if Arnolphe and M. Jourdain are human, so is their creator; and though we may be conscious of too much kinship with their vanity and folly, we have a right also to remember that we come of the same family as Molière's perfect soundness of heart and head.

DRYDEN AND SHAKESPEARE [1]

THE Mermaid Series of plays by the old dramatists is reappearing in a new and pleasanter shape, and at last Dryden takes his proper place among his fellows and even receives the honour of two volumes instead of one. It is strange enough that room was not found for him from the first, considering that the collection stretched from Marlowe to Vanbrugh and Steele, and therefore covered the period when Dryden's was considered as much the first English name in the drama as in other forms of literature. But perhaps it was just his many-sidedness that undid him. To be 'famed in all great arts, in none supreme' is never perhaps in literature the way to the most permanent sort of glory. The smaller star pales before the greater, and, in Dryden's case, the poems have extinguished the plays. Yet that should not be so; and lovers of good literature will be glad of anything which, like the issue of these two volumes, may tend to avert it. For the plays are full, in the first place, of that wonderful 'literary craftsmanship' on which Professor Saintsbury well insists as so great a quality in Dryden. And they are full also of that fine gift of ease, measure, and good sense which made him so admirable in prose and yet never overcame the poet in him. A little before his day the poet had been all a poet, or at least all a man of letters; a little later he is all a man of the world and the town. But in Dryden, study and parlour and tavern all play their parts, and the poet talks the language of polite society without letting his sense or wit extinguish his fire.

[1] *John Dryden.* Edited with an Introduction and Notes by George Saintsbury. Two vols. The Mermaid Series. Unwin.

And all this is in the plays as it is elsewhere. But the greatest of reasons why they ought to be remembered is simply that among their number is *All for Love*. The whole of a family shares in the glory of its one great son, and Dryden's other plays have only to say they are by the author of *All for Love* to find themselves at any time in the best company and very honourably treated. But, on the whole, it will not be for their own sake. ' I was tragedian in that scene alone' might almost have come from the mouth of Dryden a hundred and fifty years before it uttered the proud humility of Landor.

The new edition contains eight plays—*All for Love*, the two *Conquests of Granada, Aureng-Zebe, The Spanish Friar, Don Sebastian, Albion and Albanius,* and *Marriage à la Mode.* They are chosen and edited by Professor Saintsbury, the editor of the last edition of Scott's great Dryden, and probably the greatest living authority on the poet. Is there any other living man who has read all that Dryden wrote many times, as he seems to have done ? That is at any rate the best foundation a critic can have, and, indeed, sheer learning is everywhere the strong point of Mr. Saintsbury's criticism. In actual acquaintance with the good, bad, and indifferent *belles lettres* of England and France he can have very few rivals, and the interesting introduction to the present books shows not only the too-familiar eccentricities of the critic's style, but also the old variety and reality of learning. He is always the scholar without the gown ; and when scholars put off their gowns, they are apt to go more naked than other people who never had gowns, as may be seen in the case of the greatest of Oxford scholars of the last generation, who wrote quite cheerfully in his memoirs that ' a country squire or rector, on landing with his cub under his wing in Oxford, finds himself much at sea '. It would be better, however, if this slippered ease was regarded solely as a posthumous privilege to which

Mr. Saintsbury is happily not yet entitled. Still, with or
without a gown he is always a scholar, and Dryden can wish
for no better sponsor to introduce him to modern readers.

The real importance, however, of these two pleasant and
handy volumes lies neither in the instructive introduction
nor in anything else they contain, but in the fact that they
put the best plays of Dryden, and, above all, the incomparable *All for Love*, for the first time within the reach of
the ordinary buyer of books. The fashion of making literary
parallels, for contrast or comparison, is one that has rather
passed away. Homer and Virgil, the *Iliad* and the *Odyssey*,
Paradise Lost and *Paradise Regained*—we have now learnt
to enjoy them all and allow each man his own merits without complaining that he has not those of some one else. But
there was some real sense and interest in the practice, if it
could keep free from the Whig and Tory spirit that infected
it too often. The use of the Opposition is to bring out the
faults of the Ministry; they have nothing to do with its
merits. But the literary critic is a judge whose summing
up ought to give the strong points of both plaintiff and
defendant. And when that is fairly done, or even honestly
attempted, these literary parallels are not without their
interest or their use. And in English literature there is not
one more interesting than that between *Antony and Cleopatra*
and *All for Love*.

The points of resemblance are, of course, obvious enough.
The subject of both is the most famous of the world's love
stories, and it is more than a mere community of subject,
which has often existed between writers who never heard of
each other. The principal source Dryden used in writing his
play was not Plutarch or Appian or Dion Cassius; it was
Shakespeare himself. 'In my style I have professed to
imitate the divine Shakespeare'; and 'I hope I may affirm,
and without vanity, that, by imitating him, I have excelled
myself throughout the play'. So he tells us in his Preface,

with noble modesty, in a day when men in general were still too near that mountain known as Shakespeare to realize its towering and unapproachable height. Yet the imitation is no slavish one. It owes much, but far from all, to its original. What did it receive and what does it bring? Well, there are some things that are receivable and some that are not. *Demens qui nimbos et non imitabile fulmen*, the eternal epitaph of those who do not know their place, would be the inevitable verdict on the fool who should try to retouch the unique incommunicable things of Shakespeare. No other man in the history of the world could quite have given us ' the baby at my breast, that sucks the nurse asleep'; other people who know their business will just let that alone for ever. And, though that stands by itself, the play has a good many other things of that high sort which meant death to the profane toucher. What is any other poet to do with ' Where's my serpent of old Nile?' or with the ' morsel cold upon dead Caesar's trencher', or with ' O withered is the garland of the war', or the passages of which they are merely the central jewels, except just to wonder and be silent? Who will need the warning voice to cry, ' touch not, taste not, handle not '?

Yet there is a good deal that Dryden found he could steal with honour and profit, and he has not feared to do so. But he has not forgotten that the poor are not entitled to more than the crumbs from the rich man's table. Many fragments will make one mouthful for him. Take such a passage as his

> There's no satiety of love in thee :
> Enjoyed, thou still art new : perpetual spring
> Is in thy arms : the ripened fruit but falls,
> And blossoms rise to fill its empty place :
> And I grow rich by giving.

It begins, of course, with a reminiscence of the incomparable ' Age cannot wither her, nor custom stale Her infinite variety'; but, as if to avoid direct rivalry with the magician,

Dryden has transferred it to the mouth of Antony himself;
and then it is mingled with gleanings from another great
passage that Shakespeare had given to Cleopatra:—

> For his bounty
> There was no winter in't: an autumn 'twas
> That grew the more by reaping:

and so the whole is put together and made the fine thing it
is. Then, again, he could not pass over the great scene of
Cleopatra in the barge. And he has borrowed well and
wisely taking what was in him to take, avoiding the
Shakespearean conceits, and making a picture which is at
once splendid and, even if avowedly after Shakespeare, still
undoubtedly painted in his own manner. No one can do
better such a thing as

> To soft flutes
> The silver oars kept time; and while they played,
> The hearing gave new pleasure to the sight;
> And both to thought.

But he dare not turn a bare word of Plutarch into such
a picture as that of Antony alone in the deserted city
'enthroned i' the market-place' and 'whistling to the air';
and, if he is without Shakespeare's extravagances, he is
equally without that lavish and royal exuberance which
in Shakespeare makes every line ring with the reckless
splendour of Cleopatra.

But if there is so much in Dryden that is borrowed, and
so much more that it is his misfortune he could not borrow,
how is it that *All for Love* is, after all, as some are bold
enough to think, even more difficult to put down unfinished
than *Antony and Cleopatra*? Broadly speaking, the answer
is very simple. *Antony and Cleopatra* is drama in the shape
of chronicle, *All for Love* is drama in the shape of drama.
There is nothing Shakespeare could not do, when he chose;
but even he, when he achieves the impossible, cannot get
rid of all traces of the impossibility. And no occasional

triumphs of genius will alter the fact that the drama is a
confined form of literature and not an unconfined, that its
field can never be all time, all place, and all existence, as that
of the epic may almost be said to be, but that, other things
being equal, it will succeed the better the closer it keeps to
one time, one place, and one existence. There we get, of
course, to the old battle of those famous unities, so long
regarded in England as a mere piece of French pedantry.
It is, no doubt, easy to exaggerate their importance ; but it
is easier still to exaggerate their unimportance. For see
what they can do in such a case as the one before us.
Nothing on earth, of course, could make Dryden Shakespeare's equal. But a small man working with the right tools
will get nearer to a big man working with the wrong, than
if both worked with the right or both with the wrong. These
are relative words, of course, but one really need not go outside Shakespeare to see what a difference those derided
unities, or rather the one important one, that of action or
interest, can make. Why has *Othello* been thought by good
judges to be the most moving play he wrote ? Surely, not
only for Desdemona's sake, but, if we think it out, because
the action is more completely one than in any of the other
tragedies. Why, again, do the great tragedies *Lear*, *Hamlet*,
Macbeth take so much more complete possession of our whole
being than the great Histories, *Julius Caesar*, or *Henry IV*,
or this *Antony and Cleopatra* ? For the same reason: that because these last are histories, they must be imperfect tragedies ;
for history and tragedy are not the same thing. No Falstaff
or Brutus, or Cleopatra can quite compensate for that defect.
For the drama has but a short time to do its work in, and to
get it done the dramatist is wise to look neither to the right
hand nor to the left, but to keep his eyes and ours fixed only
on Hamlet's ' necessary question of the play'.

Many people, inclined to look on art and law as the enemies
instead of the instruments of genius, will think this over-

strict doctrine. To those who do may be commended the question, why Dryden in *All for Love* comes so much nearer Shakespeare than would naturally have been expected ? Can they avoid the answer that it is not only that from his closeness to Shakespeare in this play he caught something of a spirit greater than his own, but also that he refused to load himself with encumbrances which make even Shakespeare's fiery energy reach the goal with difficulty, and would have prevented Dryden from reaching it at all ? Who has not felt obliged in reading *Antony and Cleopatra* to turn back in bewilderment to the list of *dramatis personae*, as one unimportant personage after another fills the stage ? Dryden is rid of that confusion at once : he has ten characters for Shakespeare's thirty-four. Then Shakespeare's action occupies twelve years, and takes place in about twelve different scenes; Dryden's all takes place at Alexandria, and in a few hours. But that is of less importance. The thing that makes the great difference is that *All for Love* is really what its name implies ; whatever is said, done, or suffered, belongs to the love of Antony and to Cleopatra, and to nothing else at all. Here we have no Pompey or Lepidus, no rivalries of Triumvirs, no political intrigue, no superfluous or semi-superfluous scenes like some half-dozen or dozen of those in Shakespeare's play ; here the circumference never forgets its centre, 'every scene,' as Dryden says, 'conducing to the main design, and every Act concluding with a turn of it'; all moves forward steadily to the catastrophe, and we never for a moment lose sight of the immortal passion which is the whole of *All for Love*, the beginning and the middle and the end.

If we read the two plays with open minds, and are resolute to keep on this side idolatry in our thoughts of Shakespeare, it will surely be plain that in this matter of art and handling it is Dryden and not Shakespeare who has shown the sounder judgement. Shakespeare, in spite of his by-paths, may arrive first at the goal; but Dryden, by virtue of his straight road, is not so immeasurably far behind him. Nor is that his only virtue. Those who love fine things need not be afraid that *All for Love* will give them nothing but a well-designed general composition. It is full of glorious lines and brave sayings. Here, indeed, we must not think of Shakespeare; but, if we do not, will it not need some searching to find better things than Dolabella's

> Heaven has but
> Our sorrow for our sins.

or, in a very different vein, Antony's

> Let furies drag thee quick to hell; let all
> The longer damned have rest; each torturing hand
> Do thou employ, till Cleopatra comes.

or, again, Antony's grief—

> Then, art thou innocent, my poor dear love,
> And art thou dead?
> O those two words! their sound should be divided:
> Hadst thou been false, and died; or hadst thou lived,
> And hadst been true—But innocence and death!
> This shows not well above.

The thing in which Dryden hardly ever fails is his literary craftsmanship; but such things as these, and there are not a few of them, are enough to show that he had something in him which no mere art or training can ever give.

COLLINS AND GRAY [1]

POETRY has often been compared to gold, but there is at least one obvious point in which the comparison signally fails. It is impossible to value poetry by its weight. Exuberance of production does, indeed, generally help a poet's fame in his lifetime; but in the ultimate judgement it has very little part. Few of the many examples which might be adduced to prove this are more striking than the fact that the two men who, of all the professed poets in England during the age of Pope, produced, perhaps, the least and cared least about public fame and applause, are now better remembered by lovers of poetry than any of their rivals. Neither Gray nor Collins has left us in his whole works many more lines than are to be found in the *Essay on Man* or a single book of *The Seasons*. Yet Gray has probably fifty readers and Collins five for every reader of Pope or Thomson to-day. It is not that Pope and Thomson are in any danger of being forgotten. The taste of the nineteenth century has, it is true, condemned the whole manner of the one at the just judgement-seat of the imagination, and the genuine poetry of the other has been to a large extent superseded by that of greater men. But Pope's splendid gifts, unequalled in their peculiar way in the whole history of literature, make it certain that his name will never fall into oblivion, and no poet who has loved nature as Thomson loved her has ever been allowed altogether to miss his reward. Even so, however, and this is the point, neither Pope nor Thomson wrote an *Elegy* or an *Ode to Evening*; and therefore for us now, whatever

---

[1] *The Poems of William Collins.* Edited by Christopher Stone. Frowde.

their contemporary vogue, whatever their fertility of production, they do not rank at all as high in the kingdom of
pure poetry as Gray, who, we know, 'never spoke out,' or as
Collins, who spoke so softly, and so little, that his own
generation was scarcely aware that he had spoken at all.

The two men have constantly been coupled together.
Mr. Swinburne has denounced this assimilation as 'fatally
foolish and uncritical', but it will probably continue in
spite of his protest. The superficial resemblances, if there
were nothing more, would always make it convenient. In
certain obvious ways Gray and Collins stood near each other
and apart from the other poets of their day. Both were
scholars, though, of course, Collins has no pretensions to
equal Gray in this respect. Both wrote odes in a day when
lyric poetry was not in fashion; and neither of them wrote
much else. Both ostentatiously avoided the social and
satirical poetry which was the reigning taste of the day;
and both, if we put the *Elegy* out of account, were found
guilty by the reigning criticism of 'harshness and obscurity',
and of a perverse 'quest of mistaken beauties'. These are
words applied by Johnson to the work of his friend Collins,
of whom he wished to speak as tenderly as he could. Of
Gray, who was not his friend, and who had enjoyed much
more fame than ever fell to the lot of Collins, he says, as is
well known, much the same thing at the greater length,
inspired by personal animosity and perhaps by impatience
at a celebrity gained in the critic's despite.

All these circumstances considered, it is pretty certain
that Collins and Gray will continue to be often mentioned
in the same breath. And most readers of poetry will think,
in spite of Mr. Swinburne, that the two poets have more
essential things than these in common. According to
Mr. Swinburne—his study of Collins is to be found in
Mr. Humphry Ward's admirable *English Poets*—Gray 'as
an elegiac poet holds for all ages to come his unassailable

and sovereign station : as a lyric poet he is simply unworthy
to sit at the feet of Collins '. Collins, again, was 'a born
lyric poet ', while Gray 'had been made one, though self-
made '. And the critic completes his praise of Collins by
declaring that 'in the little book of odes which dropped,
a stillborn immortal, from the press . . . there was hardly
a single false note '. We are all used to Mr. Swinburne's
magisterial pronouncements in these matters; we know
that if he is for acquittal the prisoner is an angel, and if he
is for conviction the counsel for the defence is a fool. Still,
when a great poet speaks about his own art, wise people
will differ from him with reluctance and self-distrust. In
this case, however, a curious circumstance comes to reassure
the modest person who finds himself honestly unable to take
these judgements as final. The poet who follows Collins in
Mr. Ward's book is Gray; and the preface to the selection
from Gray is again written by a poet, and this time by one
whose critical gift was admittedly only second in importance
to his gift of poetry. Matthew Arnold's study of Gray is
one of the best things he did in this way, going, as his
studies always did, below the surface of circumstance and
accomplishment to the essential depths of character, to the
things that really make a poet, or any man, what he
eternally is. Only one thing, however, in that essay directly
concerns us here. It is that, after giving his view of Gray's
poetic work and contrasting it with other poetry of that
day, the critic adds 'He is alone or almost alone (for Collins
has something of the like merit) in his age '. *For Collins
has something of the like merit.* These eight words make
it obvious that Arnold differed from Mr. Swinburne very
decidedly in two points. It is clear that he thought Gray
and Collins were poets of the same order, naturally and
reasonably linked together; and it is clear that he thought
it was Gray and not Collins who must be given the higher
place.

How are those who are neither great poets nor great critics to choose their path between these opposing authorities? The only way, one supposes, is to go back to the facts, that is, to the actual poems themselves. A pleasant excuse for doing so is furnished by Mr. Christopher Stone's edition of Collins. There is not a great deal that is new in it. Of that there is no chance, unless some new letters or some of the poems said to have been destroyed by the poet's sister, Mrs. Sempill, were somehow to come to light. Mr. Stone prefaces the poems by a memoir which gives all the available information about Collins and his work; but of actually new features in the book we have noticed only a useful list of the editions of Collins, some variations of text, and the omission of the *Lines to Miss Aurelia C—r*, which Dr. Birkbeck Hill proved to have been erroneously ascribed to Collins. There are, perhaps, only two criticisms to be made on Mr. Stone's work. One is that his remarks have sometimes the obscurity of carelessness, as, for instance, when he says of the variations in the Dodsley versions of two of the odes, 'the question of their authenticity is crepuscular,' and says it in such a way that the hasty reader is as likely to apply it to the odes themselves as to the variations. Another is that he has left the very frequent errors of punctuation in the early editions uncorrected and even unnoted. The *Ode on the Poetical Character* begins in this as in earlier editions:—

> As once, if not with light Regard,
> I read aright that gifted Bard.

Surely it is not asking too much of an editor who has no chance, as in this case, of doing much else for his author, at least to deliver him from such obstructions as the comma after 'Regard', noting its previous existence, for safety's sake, if necessary. And perhaps Mr. Stone, who confesses the obscurities of his poet, would have done well to help us, here and there, by an attempt at elucidation.

Leaving these editorial questions, however, we may go back to Collins and the question of his poetic position. And, first, as to the false notes which Mr. Swinburne finds in Gray but not in Collins. Let us go to the facts. Here is the opening of one of the odes of Collins,

> While, lost to all his former Mirth,
> Britannia's Genius bends to Earth,
>   And mourns the fatal Day:
> While stained with Blood he strives to tear
> Unseemly from his Sea-Green Hair
>   The Wreaths of cheerful May.

Is it possible seriously to say, in the presence of this and many similar passages, that 'the fanfaronade and falsetto' which Mr. Swinburne finds in Gray are 'all but impossible to the finer touch of his precursor'? The question surely answers itself. Passages such as this, and such flatter absurdities as those two lines in *The Passions*—

> Brown Exercise rejoiced to hear
> And Sport leapt up, and seized his Beechen Spear,

show that Collins no more than Gray, indeed even less, could always escape the atmosphere of the eighteenth century. Neither of them was happy in it; both wished to escape—in their moments of inspiration both did actually escape—into truth and poetry; but in their uninspired moments, when only the will to escape was present and not the power, the result was neither truth nor poetry, but their too-frequent eighteenth-century substitute—rhetorical falsetto.

But this is, after all, only the negative side of their resemblance. Where is the positive? Take the opening of the finest poem Collins has left us, one of the most beautiful odes in any language:—

> If aught of Oaten Stop or Pastoral Song
> May hope, Chaste Eve, to soothe thy modest Ear,
>   Like thy own solemn Springs
>   Thy Springs and dying Gales,
> O Nymph reserved—

or take some lines that come later;

> be mine the Hut
> That from the Mountain's Side
> Views Wilds, and swelling Floods,

> And Hamlets brown, and dim-discovered Spires,
> And hears their simple Bell, and marks o'er all
> Thy dewy Fingers draw
> The gradual dusky Veil.

Is not this Gray's very atmosphere, a setting of the mood of his *Elegy* into the form of an ode ?   Is there not a degree of kinship between this and such things as—

> Now fades the glimmering landscape on the sight,
> And all the air a solemn stillness holds,

which is not to be found between either of them and the work of any other poet of that day, even that of Dyer which has some kindred qualities ? Still, of course, there is the important difference that Gray's poem is an elegy and not an ode, while the *Ode to Evening* is an ode and not an elegy.

That brings us close to a further point made by Mr. Swinburne. 'Here was at last a poet,' he says of Collins, 'who was content to sing out what he had in him—to sing and not to say, without a glimpse of wit or a flash of eloquence.' Well, perhaps, those 'two valuable and admirable superfluities', as he calls them, might be shown to be by no means so entirely absent from the work of Collins as Mr. Swinburne declares. But the 'singing not saying' is the more important point. And here, no doubt, one master of music has instantly recognized another. It is possible to read and enjoy both Gray and Collins without actually taking note of this difference, but when it has been once pointed out it is not possible to deny that there is a music in Collins at his best which is never to be found in Gray. The noble opening of the *Ode to Liberty*,

Who shall awake the Spartan Fife,

and, above all, of course, the incomparable rise and fall of
the blank verse stanzas of the *Ode to Evening* have a sheer
beauty of sound and motion in them which is not to be
found in Gray. That is going a long way towards saying
that Collins is the greater poet. But not the whole way.
Music is much, but it is not all. 'The special faculty of the
poet,' said Johnson, 'is that of joining music with reason';
which is the other side of Dryden's 'Music is inarticulate
poetry'. To become poetry, that is, music has to become
articulate; it has to add Johnson's 'reason'; it has, in fact,
to say something as well as to sing. In music the notes are
everything; even if they are given in words, as in a song,
the notes still remain more important than the words. But
in poetry the words are at least as important as the notes,
because the poet has to unite reason with music, has to
address the mind, and not merely the ear. Now is it not in
this direction that the explanation is to be sought of what
seems so strange to Mr. Swinburne, the fact that many
people think Gray a greater lyrical poet than Collins?
Gray, after all, wrote odes, and he himself thought, as
Matthew Arnold followed him in thinking, that among
them, and not in the *Elegy*, was to be found his best poetic
work. Whether that be so or not, and whether or not any of
his odes is as great a performance as the *Ode to Evening*, it
remains true that he is more read than Collins, and for
a very simple reason; there is more in him. He covers
far more ground, he says more, he interests more. Perhaps
he never satisfies so perfectly, never leaves us resting quite
so completely content as that single masterpiece of Collins;
but, on the other hand, far more of his lines possess that
combined truth of observation and felicity of expression
which the memory finds irresistible. It is not only that
the *Elegy* is a mass of quotations; but who forgets such
things as

> But chief, the skylark warbles high
> His trembling thrilling ecstacy;
> And, lessening from the dazzled sight,
> Melts into air and liquid light;

or a thing very different, the Miltonic praise of Milton in the *Progress of Poesy*; or, again, such admirable gnomic lines as

> And leave us leisure to be good?

These are everywhere in Gray. He had tenderness enough, as the *Elegy*, and the wonderful alcaic fragment *O lacrimarum fons*, would be alone sufficient to prove. But his real superiority, as compared with Collins, lies in his being able to bring so much more mind to bear on the subjects he took for his poems. The contrast is well seen in their two odes on Poetry itself. Gray is learned, stimulating, vigorous, full of power of imagination, of power of thought, of power of expression. He leaves us dazzled with his 'thoughts that breathe and words that burn', delighted with his *curiosa felicitas* of language, interested with his critical judgements. The ode of Collins is an altogether smaller performance. It is by no means his finest work. But it gives both sides of the comparison with Gray very well. It has no pretensions to Gray's energy and power. There is nothing in it of Gray's sweeping range, of his splendid colour, of his high instinct for language, of his fine sense for the composition of a great work of art. It is the performance of a younger and weaker mind, one that has read less and thought less, one that has less in it. These are defects that will always tell, and, in fact, deserve always to tell. In all probability they will always have enough influence to make Collins a less popular poet than Gray. But there is also the other side of the picture in the *Ode on the Poetical Character*. The greater simplicity of Collins saves him from any such jarring piece of affected antithesis as that with which Gray's Ode ends :—

Beneath the Good how far—but far above the Great.

And it is, perhaps, not altogether an accident that the one poet writes on The Progress of Poesy, a chronicle, as it were, of its external triumphs, the other on The Poetical Character, an attempt to penetrate to the uniqueness of the mystery of Poetry, to

Gaze her Visions wild, to feel unmix'd her Flame.

Nor is it quite without possible significance that while each poet concludes by a modest disclaimer of any hope of these high poetic glories for himself, Gray turns for final consolation to the thought of moral achievement—

Yet shall he mount, and keep his distant way
Beyond the limits of a vulgar fate;—

but Collins has his eye fixed to the last on the poetic vision, and on that alone, or the place where it was, when the vision itself has disappeared into darkness and despair.

In vain—Such Bliss to One alone,
Of all the Sons of Soul, was known,
And Heaven, and Fancy, kindred Powers,
Have now o'erturned th' inspiring Bowers,
Or curtained close such Scene from every future View.

May not that be the truth? Collins had the purer vein of poetry in him; but *abstulit atra dies,* fate and circumstances were against him, and to Gray, with the less original poetic faculty, remains the glory of the greater achievement.

JOHNSON WITHOUT BOSWELL [1]

IT was apparently Burke who first remarked that Johnson
was greater in Boswell's book than he had been in his own;
and this has gradually come to be the almost universal
opinion. The vogue of Macaulay is not what it was, but he
still plays a great part in stimulating the enjoyment and
forming the opinions of those who are just beginning to care
about books; and the least objectionable thing in one of his
worst essays is its exaltation of Johnson's talk at the expense
of his writings. Nor is there any need to quarrel with this
preference. Indeed, the slowly accumulating certainty of
time gathers more and more to its support. There will never
be an edition of Johnson in shilling parts such as that Messrs.
Pitman are issuing of Boswell with 400 excellent illustrations. Not many people read *The Rambler* at all now, and
no one reads it often or even all through. Every one reads
Boswell, and wise men, like Jowett, read him fifty times.

This is so, and there are good reasons why it should be so.
Books are written to be read, and, in the long run, they will
be read only in proportion as they are readable. Boswell's
Life is one of the most readable books in all the world, and
no one will say that of *Rasselas* or of *The Rambler*. Still,
it must not be forgotten that the quality of readableness
depends upon the reader. The poet Ronsard would not
leave his house till he had finished the *Iliad*, and living
enthusiasts have been known to forget their luncheon over

---

[1] *Samuel Johnson.* The Leslie Stephen Lecture. Delivered in the
Senate House, Cambridge. By Walter Raleigh. Oxford: Clarendon
Press. *Selections from Dr. Johnson's 'Rambler'*. Edited, with Preface
and Notes, by W. Hale White. Oxford: Clarendon Press. *Boswell's
Johnson.* Newly edited by Roger Ingpen. 400 Illustrations. In twelve
monthly parts. Sir Isaac Pitman.

Mill's *Logic*, and even to go through *The Ring and the Book*
at a sitting. On the other hand, the easiest of good novels,
Pride and Prejudice, *The Heart of Midlothian*, even *The
Wrong Box*, are tedious to those who have dissipated their
brains and ruined their imaginations among the distracting
trivialities of the cheap Press. That, too, it may be remarked, is an acquired taste or want of taste. There never
yet was a child who did not infinitely prefer *Alice in Wonder-
land*, or, for the matter of that, a book of tales from Homer
or Shakespeare, to any newspaper. But that is by the way.
The present point is whether Johnson's works might not be
found more readable by the right readers than is generally
thought.

That is the question which Mr. Hale White's little book
ought to have helped to answer for *The Rambler*. But it
scarcely will. The truth is, to speak frankly, that it is not
quite worthy either of Johnson or of Oxford. In the first
place, its plan is unfortunate. It consists of selected passages, some of them of great length, so that it has neither
the advantages of a book of aphorisms, nor those of a book
of essays. There is a fairly large public for collections of
maxims, birthday-books, and such things, providing brief
texts in which people find energy for the activities of the
day or suggestion for the meditations of the night. And
there is another public not so large, for sermons, or essays
on serious subjects. A volume of either sort might easily
have been made out of *The Rambler*. But this is neither
the one nor the other. Who will read a book of unclassified
fragments which neither arrest by their brevity nor satisfy
by their completeness ? Nor is Mr. White's critical judgement altogether to be trusted. He says, for instance, that
Johnson's corrections in the revised edition of *The Rambler*
were 'almost always improvements', and he proceeds to give
an example in which the principal change is the substitution
of this sentence—'If he thinks his own judgment not

sufficiently enlightened, he may, by attending the remarks
which every paper will produce, rectify his opinions'—for
an earlier version which ran as follows: 'If he thinks his
own judgment not sufficiently enlightened, he may, by
attending the remarks which every paper will produce,
inform himself of his mistakes, rectify his opinions, and
extend his views.' Will any good judge regard this altera-
tion as an improvement? Both the ear and the mind suffer
by it. The poise of the sentence is entirely ruined in the
revised version: the conclusion, 'rectify his opinions,' has
no longer by itself the weight to balance all that goes before,
and is in the nature of an oral anti-climax. And the phrases
omitted were no superfluities introduced for the ear's sake.
They add to the sense. The criticisms an author receives
do more than 'rectify his opinions'; they do, or may do, two
other things: they may point out to him his mistakes, and
they may enlarge his views. It is curious that Mr. Hale
White should have failed to see this, for he himself points
out, in the course of some interesting remarks on Johnson's
style, that 'it seldom admits real surplusage, and what is
called the Johnsonian balance is not mere see-saw'. 'Each
member' of his sentences 'conveys a new idea, or is a double
stroke on the head of the nail'.

This is, in the main, a true defence of Johnson's much-
abused style. The chief fault of that style is that it cannot
do certain work which it occasionally tried to do. It cannot, for example, trifle gracefully. When it wants to make
us smile at the discomfiture of some silly young gentlemen
who went to the pit armed with cat-calls for the purpose of
making the performance impossible, it informs us that the
other spectators 'snatched away their instruments of criticism and, by the seasonable vibration of a stick, subdued them
instantaneously to decency and silence'. There is no need
to insist on the point; many people have parodied this side
of Johnson, and everybody has laughed at it. Even in his

talk there is not much lightness of touch : there is none at all in his writings. When he trifles he trifles with dignity, and therefore generally with difficulty. In fact dignity, the dignity of literature, the scholar's pride, was probably at the root of the evil. Books in his day, and particularly in his eyes, were still rather solemn things to be kept above the linguistic level of the talk of the club or the parlour. Dryden and Addison had begun to make the great discovery that the best prose style has no conscious air of literature about it ; but the new doctrine had not reached the mass either of writers or of readers. Johnson himself accidentally, as it were, gave one of the best definitions of the new style in his admirable praise of Shakespeare's comic dialogue as being, at its best, gathered from that kind of conversation which is ' above grossness and below refinement '. And he was later on to give some fine specimens of it in his *Lives of the Poets*. But he had not risen to it in his earlier days, for at that time he could never bring himself to be ' below refinement '—the refinement, not of the drawing-room, but of the library. Then, again, it cannot be denied that he has the disadvantages as well as the advantages of weight. His talk abounds in heavy-handed blows, his writings contain too many heavy-gaited sentences. Indeed, his prose is entirely lacking in lightness of touch, in mobility, in swift-ness. The swiftest of all recorded talkers, he is generally one of the slowest of writers : not that he really wrote slowly, of course, but that he appears to do so. He is encumbered on his march by a vast baggage train of learning, of thought, of meditation, of a desire to instruct and to improve. Then in our eyes he has another defect, which belongs to the whole atmosphere of his century, though it affected him more, perhaps, than any other of the great writers. He is colour-less and abstract, lacking in detail, given over-much to generalities. His style is perhaps the most striking example of the eighteenth-century love of general principles, and

disdain of the concrete detail without which general principles seem to us insipid. The least picturesque of writers,
he uses his mind a great deal more willingly than his eyes.
To him a blade of grass is a blade of grass all the world
over; and, at any rate in his earlier writings, the counters
of his argument are seldom anything that can be seen, heard,
or handled, but almost always moral or intellectual ideas.
In fact, he is one of the completest representatives of that
literature of abstractions which Scott in England and the
Romantics in France were soon to fight with all the weapons
of definitely observed shapes, sounds, and colours.

For all these reasons, and others, his prose went more and
more out of fashion throughout the nineteenth century, till
now the study of his works has even, as Mr. Raleigh says in
his pleasant and interesting Leslie Stephen lecture, acquired
'a certain flavour of novelty and research'. Yet it is impossible that Johnson should have acquired the fame he did
acquire if his writings had not possessed some of the highest
qualities that are to be found in books. It was not Boswell's
unwritten *Life* that gave him a sort of acknowledged royalty
among the men of letters of his day such as no Englishman
has held before or since. The reason why he enjoyed a great
position was that he was universally admitted to have done
great things; and no competent judge who has read the
Preface to the Dictionary, the Preface to Shakespeare, the
best of the *Lives of the Poets*, even the best of *The Rambler*,
will doubt that the verdict of his contemporaries was as just
as it was unhesitating and assured. It may be the first sign
of a salutary revival of interest in these great but neglected
works that the finest, perhaps, of living critics should make
them the subject of the first of a series of lectures which are
to be delivered every year in Cambridge, and are to bear the
name of that true lover of good literature and lifelong Johnsonian, Leslie Stephen. Mr. Raleigh is very bold, overbold
indeed, it must be confessed, in his championship. There

are wise, true, and great things in *The Rambler*; but is it not going rather far to call it as a whole 'that splendid repository of wisdom and truth'? Again, the essay on bashfulness is an admirable piece of English; but to speak of some sentences from it as 'prose that will not suffer much by comparison with the best in the language' is surely to provoke opposition and reaction. The very highest qualities of prose Johnson has not. He has not, for instance, the musical wisdom of Shakespeare, the imaginative eloquence of Burke, the picturesque and pregnant brevity of Bacon, the fervent glories of Ruskin, the vivid lightnings of Carlyle. With him prose is not what it is with these men, a voice of all but prophetic inspiration. It is a voice of great things indeed, of wide learning, of a noble seriousness, of a rare intellectual energy, of an unparalleled common sense; but of that, of the very highest, it is not a voice. But there is no need to give it praises that are not its own; for the truth is that its own are great enough, varied enough, and, in spite of temporary fashions, enduring enough to stand by themselves.

There is a story that Charlotte Brontë, when a girl of sixteen, broke out very angrily at some one who said she was always talking about clever people, such as Johnson and Sheridan. 'Now, you don't know the meaning of clever,' she said; 'Sheridan might be clever—scamps often are; but Johnson hadn't a spark of 'cleverality' in him.' That remark really gives the essence of Johnson and the key to the great qualities of his work: for, in his case, even more than in most, the prose was the man. Whoever wants 'cleverality', whoever wants what Mr. Bernard Shaw is supplying to the present generation, had best leave Johnson alone. The signal merit of Johnson's writings is that he always means what he says and always says what he means. He may often have talked for victory; but, except, perhaps in the political pamphlets, he always wrote for truth. And

what moral earnestness and intellectual energy he brought
to its service! How invariably he rises far above the mere
writer; how the author everywhere disappears in the man!
How clear he is that life is the object of learning, and not
learning the object of life! In his most scholarly moment,
in the Preface to the Dictionary, he will throw out such
a remark as, 'this recommendation of steadiness and uni-
formity (in spelling) does not proceed from an opinion that
particular combinations of letters have much influence on
human happiness.' His pedantry, if pedantry there be, is
always of manner, never of substance. Swift himself hardly
goes more directly to the business in hand. 'Obsolete words
are admitted when they are found in authors not obsolete.'
'Some words there are which I cannot explain, because I do
not understand them.' No one gives a more constant impression of frankness, manliness, and modesty. He is always
bringing fine words to the test of plain fact and common
knowledge. When Cowley, like many others before and
since, talks complacently of poverty on five hundred a year,
the answer of Johnson is the answer of common sense; 'no
man can, with any propriety, be termed poor who does not
see the greater part of mankind richer than himself.' He
cuts instantly through all intellectual cobwebs however
exquisitely woven. Truth is his measure and honesty his
knife; and no one ever had a greater horror of that pest of
literature which Joubert called 'l'ingénieux sans bon sens'.

The fine writing of his own style has been absurdly
exaggerated. It is there no doubt, but not at all to the
degree or of the sort commonly alleged. Fine writing
for fine writing's sake, adding neither information nor argument to what has been said before, is exceptionally rare in
Johnson. When he says that he knows nothing of Mallet
except what is 'supplied by the unauthorized loquacity of
common fame', it is possible to dislike the phrase; it is not
possible to deny that the words are as full of meaning as

words can be. Nor is even this at all so frequent as is
thought by those who get their notions of Johnson from
his critics. You may read many pages even of *The Rambler*
without being struck by a single instance of it; and even
where the phrase does suffer from having had to take its
paces too much from the Johnsonian drill sergeant, and to
stiffen its attitudes to the requirements of the Johnsonian
uniform, how the power of the man's mind and his self-
revealing honesty of speech break through after all, and
give human interest to what is said!

The senses have not only that advantage over conscience
which things necessary must always have over things chosen,
but they have likewise a kind of prescription in their favour.
We feared pain much earlier than we apprehended guilt,
and were delighted with the sensations of pleasure before we
had capacities to be charmed with the beauty of rectitude.
To this power, thus early established, and incessantly increasing, it must be remembered that almost every man has,
in some part of his life, added new strength by a voluntary
or negligent subjection of himself; for who is there that has
not instigated his appetites by indulgence, or suffered them
by an unresisting neutrality to enlarge their dominion and
multiply their demands?

Who does not recognize that, whatever its faults, this is the
prose of a man who has thought and felt? And there are
moments when all artificialities are cast aside, passages,
such as that in No. 54 beginning 'When a friend is carried
to his grave', in which Johnson quite forgets to put on the
scholar's gown, and that rugged heart finds utterance in
words which pass beyond eloquence into music.

But this grave moralist must not be thought to be the
only author of the works of Johnson. There is the mild
humorist of *The Idler* who sometimes gives us a very
pleasant touch, such as that which refutes the philosophic
doctrine that human life must be either active or contem-
plative by simply citing the case of maiden aunts with
small fortunes! There is the vigorous controversialist of the

political pamphlets, who is no more inclined to mince matters than Boswell's denouncer of ' bottomless Whigs ' and ' odious wenches '. The opinions may be all wrong, but that does not matter so much now ; and how many pamphlets a hundred years old are as readable as *The False Alarm*? Never was the weapon of intellectual contempt more vigorously wielded. We redouble our admiration of the Boswellian diplomacy, and our enjoyment of the dinner with Wilkes, after reading such a passage as the following :—

All wrong ought to be rectified. If Mr. Wilkes is deprived of a lawful seat, both he and his electors have reason to complain, but it will not be easily found why, among the innumerable wrongs of which a great part of mankind are hourly complaining, the whole care of the publick should be transferred to Mr. Wilkes and the freeholders of Middlesex, who might all sink into non-existence without any other effect than that there would be room made for a new rabble, and a new retailer of sedition and obscenity.

That has the smack of an evening at the Mitre about it.

But, readable as all his political talk is, it is not in that direction that we must look for the utterance of the central Johnson. Was it not Bagehot who said that it was the business of the Prime Minister in this country to have more common sense than any man? Johnson was the Prime Minister of literature. It was not his place or duty to be always originating new ideas, and some of the finest were above his ken ; but he never had his equal for gathering together the common stock of wisdom and knowledge, putting it to the test of life and truth, and applying it to the business in hand. Nothing relieves an abstract or technical discussion so much as some brief principle of general application. Of these no one is a greater master than Johnson. ' Nothing can please many, and please long, but just representations of general nature ' ; ' of men as of everything else we must judge according to our knowledge ' ; 'to be happy at home is the ultimate result of all ambition ' ; ' the sun has risen and the corn has grown, and whatever talk has been of the danger of property, yet he that ploughed the field commonly reaped it, and he that built a house was master of the door.' It is by his use of such plain sayings as these, never in his hands mere commonplaces, but things relishing fresh of life and experience, that Johnson is surest of his hold on a great place among the writers of English prose.

THE COMMEMORATION OF CRABBE

Our grandfathers stayed at home and read the poets; we run about the world to see their houses or their graves, but we have no time to open their works. Modern life seems to tend more and more, like life under the later Roman Emperors, to be swallowed up in an endless round of complimentary performances, public and private. When we are not thanking our friends, we are congratulating them; and we have scarcely dispatched our letter of congratulation before we are again seated at the writing-desk with a letter of condolence to accomplish. We post over land and sea to visit Tasso's tomb or Petrarch's fountain, Wordsworth's cottage or Goethe's birthplace. We join with the Mantuans in celebrating the memory of Virgil, with the Spaniards in honouring Don Quixote, with the Germans in keeping the centenary of Schiller. We preserve Shakespeare's birthplace and Milton's cottage as places of pilgrimage set apart in their memory for ever. But, if no one might pass up to the fountain of Vaucluse or into the cottage at Chalfont who could not quote a line of Petrarch or Milton, the number of visitors would be considerably reduced. We have in abundance, and were never so conscious of having, our

> Poets, hymns, and songs divine,

but they are in our biographical dictionaries or, at best, on our bookshelves—

> The most we read not, but allow them fine.

Let us, then, do what is permitted to a degenerate age. The little, windy, wave-beaten town where the writer of that line first saw the light does not probably contain many readers of its poet to-day, but it is, nevertheless, not altogether unaware of its single literary glory. And so for a few days now Crabbe is the centre of interest in Aldeburgh, and no longer a mere name, or a bust in a corner of the church on the hill, asked after, now and then, by an inquisitive stranger.

It was just over 150 years ago that the event took place which gives Aldeburgh its right to these celebrations. George Crabbe was born there on Christmas Eve, 1754. He was at first bred a surgeon, but that was not his destiny, and he took ship for London in 1780, with three pounds in his pocket and a literary career in his dreams. There he was fortunate enough, after some miserable months, to address himself for help to Burke, who read his letter and the verses he sent with it, and at once, with ever memorable generosity, granted him an interview and relieved his necessities; and before very long had invited him to his country house, introduced him to some of the first men of the time, and found him a publisher for his poem *The Library*. That is the only crisis in his uneventful life. When the unwearying good genius to whom he owed everything had smoothed away the difficulties that stood in the way of his wish to take orders, all the rest went as peacefully as the life of a well-to-do clergyman commonly does. On being ordained he went back in triumph to be curate at Aldeburgh; but Aldeburgh, as was natural enough, was the very last place where he was likely to be accepted at the new valuation, and the unhonoured prophet left his birthplace after a few months to become chaplain to the Duke of Rutland at Belvoir. It was Burke once more who had been the fairy godmother of this new piece of good fortune. Crabbe went to Belvoir in 1782, married in 1783, removed to a curacy near Belvoir in 1785, and from that year till his death in 1832 lived the life of a country clergyman, first as rector of Muston, in Leicestershire, then in Suffolk as curate of Sweffling and Great Glemham from 1792 to 1805, then again at Muston from 1805 to 1814, and finally, after his wife's death, at Trowbridge where his own death took place.

But it is, after all, the poet, and not the clergyman, whom Aldeburgh is celebrating this week. What we remember about Crabbe now is that he wrote *The Village*, *The Parish Register*, and, above all, the great Tales. He did not himself, indeed, take much trouble to be known as a poet, at least during his most vigorous years. Between 1783, when he achieved a great success with *The Village*, and 1807, when *The Parish Register* appeared, he published no verse at all. And by then he had missed his chance. *The Borough*, the *Tales*, and the *Tales of the Hall*, came too late. With Cowper he might perhaps have disputed the palm of popularity. There could be no disputing it with Scott and Byron. A new world of poetry had been born, and he belonged to the old.

That is, perhaps, the impression he is most certain to make on the ordinary modern reader of poetry. He is old-fashioned. He who lived thirty years longer than Cowper is much less modern than the best of Cowper. He who lived through the first generation of the nineteenth century belongs entirely to the eighteenth. This is so both in manner and in substance. His verse is his own, of course, and no one else's, or he would not be a poet at all; but it belongs to a school which has, at least for the present, definitely passed away. It is the rhymed couplet, not skilfully hiding its couplet structure as Keats and his successors hide it, but insisting on it, glorying in it, using it as the most effective of all weapons for satire and epigram and wit. Its language is not, indeed, the artificial 'Shepherdess' language so common between Dryden and Wordsworth; but neither is it the language of austere simplicity, great by association with great deeds and high emotions, which the example of Wordsworth recovered for us. At its worst, it is the ordinary language of ordinary people at ordinary moments. At its best, its praise is more often that of terseness, pregnancy, and truth, less often that of any moving or haunting quality such as we now look for in poets. And if we, brought up on Wordsworth and Coleridge, Shelley and Keats, feel a long way off a kind of verse which gives us measure when we look for music and the language of its own day when we look for the language of all days, we find the matter of Crabbe's poetry almost as strange to us as its manner. His tales have all sorts of admirable qualities ; but the atmosphere in which they are set, their moral atmosphere, is often one which our generation no longer easily understands. Crabbe's knowledge of human character is his especial distinction. And yet when we read his tales, while we are interested, moved, even delighted, there is yet again and again something that puzzles us, something that we feel to be lacking. This powerful painter of the human story, this stern judge who is yet so merciful, what is it that we vaguely feel he wants ? Is it not that in all his judgements, harsh or gentle, there is felt to be a kind of 'cool reasonableness' which belongs to the age of Addison and Bishop Butler and Johnson and no longer to ours? Or take his marriages. They are commonly of the sort that would be universal if Johnson had had his way and every man's wife were selected for him by the well-considering wisdom of the Lord Chancellor. It is a sort which very likely includes the best of all. But it is not the sort which we now think of as the natural theme of poetry. Crabbe, in fact, for all his strong feelings and active sympathies, still lives in the world of the moral essayists. His morality is rational and not emotional at all. But Wordsworth taught the nineteenth century to believe in the emotions ; and it has not forgotten the lesson.

Why, then, with all these limitations, is Crabbe to be

remembered at Aldeburgh, or elsewhere? What is it that
made Burke his enthusiastic admirer; that made Fox read
him constantly, read him on his deathbed after he could read
nothing else; that made Scott take him up more often than
any poet except Shakespeare, and call for him in the last
sad weeks at Abbotsford when he called for no other book
except the Bible; that made Byron speak of him, in 1820,
as 'the first of living poets'; and, most remarkable of all,
made Wordsworth, sincerest and most sparing of praisers,
declare in 1834 that his poems, 'from their combined merits
as poetry and truth, would last full as long as anything that
has been expressed in verse since they first made their appearance'? Such admiration from such men evidently means
that there must be something wrong with any definitions
of poetry that leave Crabbe outside. When the finest theory
of poetry that ever was has been set forth, a wise man will
cheerfully defy it in such company as this. The truth is,
perhaps, that there has been loss as well as gain in the
higher conception of the poet's function which came in with
Wordsworth and has lasted ever since. In the eighteenth
century a new poem was almost as much read and quite as
much talked about as a new novel. Poetry was to be found
in every inn parlour; it was quoted at every dinner-party
of cultivated men. All the educated felt entitled to an
opinion upon it, especially upon the goodness or badness of
the verses. The art of composition played then a far greater
part in school life than it does now; and all who had had
the experience of making, or seeing others make, a well-
turned Latin verse enjoyed sitting in judgement on the merits
or demerits of verses in their own language. And not only
were there more people who had an inkling into the mystery
of verse-making and a pleasure in discussing it : the subjects
then handled by poetry were such as many more people
could understand. No doubt the *Moral Satires, The Traveller*,
and *The Village* are poetry of a lower sort than the *Ode on*

Intimations of Immortality, or the *Hymn to Intellectual Beauty*. But they had the advantage of interesting every intelligent man in England. Is there not a danger of poetry becoming a kind of specialism, which only people of a definitely imaginative turn of mind feel called upon to touch? Is it inevitable that after a century of great poetry and high imagination there should no longer be any room for the old pleasure in good sense and good verse?

That is a question too large to pursue; but there, at any rate, is the essence of Crabbe; good sense and good verse, a rare knowledge of the smaller ways of human character, a keen eye for the smaller doings of nature. English landscape was never so loved as it is to-day, and the everlasting human comedy never had more students. Crabbe is a master of both. Of the lowlands, that is, in both cases. Heights and depths, whether moral or physical, are not his province. But when he keeps to the level land, as he generally does, he knows every inch of the ground. It is the business of poetry to add the touch of life and pleasure to old sights and sounds that, till it came, were mere dull facts and nothing more. Who does it better than Crabbe for his Suffolk fields and waters? Let the people who fill Aldeburgh and Felixstowe to-day look over the description in *Peter Grimes* of the typical Suffolk river, with its low-tide stretch of gull-haunted mud and seaweed, where the eels played in the shallows,

And the loud bittern, from the bullrush home,
Gave from the salt-ditch side the bellowing boom;

and the next time they take a sail on the Orwell or the Deben they will see a great deal they never saw before and delight in all sorts of things which hitherto they have only seen. And before they start out again along the pleasant Suffolk roads on their feet or their bicycles, let them take up *The Lover's Journey*, and not only enjoy its finely told tale, but by the help of it get eyes to see—as Crabbe saw them over the hedges, and with his loving interest—the

> . . . unnumbered cottages and farms
> That have for musing minds unnumbered charms.

His poems are everywhere full of touches of this sort, waking to delighted activity dormant senses and sympathies. The magic, indeed, of Nature, or her mystery, it is not in him to give; but who can better give us the pleasure of our everyday companionship with her? And there are many days when we ask for nothing more. Where is it better given than in such a passage as that at the opening of the *Tales of the Hall* where the elder brother returns to settle in his native place? It is one in which the poet's rough edges are for once all smoothed away, till it closes on a note of almost Spenserian sweetness.

> He chose his native village and the hill
> He climb'd a boy had its attraction still;
> With that small brook beneath, where he would stand
> And stooping fill the hollow of his hand
> To quench th' impatient thirst—then stop awhile
> To see the sun upon the waters smile,
> In that sweet weariness, when, long denied,
> We drink and view the fountain that supplied
> The sparkling bliss—and feel, if not express,
> Our perfect ease in that sweet weariness.

Truth and poetry; there are both in Crabbe, as Wordsworth said. Every one has felt the pleasure of satisfied thirst as a fact; every one who has read these lines has felt it also as poetry.

The other side of Crabbe is the novelist in verse. Here, again, he certainly receives far less recognition than he deserves. Everybody reads novels nowadays, and everybody professes to like watching the play of character. Well, few novelists have had such an eye as Crabbe for the small things that are always playing their great part in the shifts and turns of the human comedy. It is not surprising that

Jane Austen said she could have married him. They have
a great deal in common, and stretch friendly hands across
the gulf that separates prose and verse. She had not poetry
enough in her, one suspects, to get the full pleasure out of
The Lover's Journey, his masterpiece ; but how she must
have enjoyed *Delay Has Danger* and *The Old Bachelor*, and
Procrastination and *The Frank Courtship*! And how another
great novelist, the greatest of the living, must, one would
imagine, delight in *Sir Owen Dale*, who is, indeed, his own
Egoist in little! Certainly both would appreciate a hundred
fine bits of observation in every story. No novelist ever
painted the unconscious growth of a love affair better than
it is done in *Delay Has Danger*. No one, again, ever sur-
passed Crabbe in a certain gift of playing pleasantly on the
surface of a variety of old maids and old bachelors. How
well he puts little humorous touches such as the beginning
of the last of the old Bachelor's adventures with the
other sex!

> Time after time the maid went out and in,
> Ere love was yet beginning to begin ;
> The first awakening proof, the early doubt,
> Rose from observing she went in and out.

Murray's remark about his talk is true also of his poetry.
He says his 'uncommon things' with so little air of their
being uncommon that they pass half unnoticed. Yet how
good they often are! The note about the young critic,
for instance, learning to despise his boyhood's favourite
books—

> Pleased with the pride that will not let them please,

or that fine distinction in *Lady Barbara* between the two
kinds of marriage :—

> And we were happy, for our love was calm,
> Not life's delicious essence, but its balm :

or the Wordsworthian touch at the end of the *Adventures of*

Richard, where the lover trembles at the excess of his own happiness, and finds its cure:—

> Such was the blessing that I sought for pain,
> In some degree to be myself again ;
> And when we met a shepherd old and lame,
> Cold and diseased, it seemed my blood to tame ;
> And I was thankful for the moral sight,
> That soberized the vast and wild delight.

Or, once more, the fine observation that lies behind the Homeric simile at the end of *Smugglers and Poachers*, with its picture of the woman who had seen her unloved husband and her too generously, though innocently, cherished lover, both killed, almost before her eyes, in a single night:—

> As men will children at their sports behold,
> And smile to see them, though unmoved and cold,
> Smile at the recollected games, and then
> Depart and mix in the affairs of men :
> So Rachael looks upon the world, and sees
> It cannot longer pain her, longer please :
> But just detain the passing thought, or cause
> A gentle smile of pity or applause ;
> And then the recollected soul repairs
> Her slumbering hope, and heeds her own affairs.

No old-fashioned surface of literary manners can stand in our way when we come to a passage like this. Only poets write such things. Only a true poet gives us back the human spectacle with this compelling sympathy that whispers somehow in the very movement of these lines. And, though this last mark of the great poet is rare in Crabbe, the knowledge and the sympathy behind it are not rare.

Fox and Wordsworth, then, and their company were right; and Newman and FitzGerald, unlike, perhaps, in everything else, were alike right in reading and loving Crabbe all their lives through; and Aldeburgh is right to-day in counting it a glory to have been his birthplace.

THE TRAGIC DRAMA, AND
ESPECIALLY ALFIERI [1]

WE have sometimes been tempted to envy France her
provincial Universities. An Englishman cannot but be
struck with surprise when he finds such books as M. Legouis's
Wordsworth or M. Huchon's *Crabbe* proceeding from places
like Nancy or Lyon ; and he regretfully thinks of the intellectual life to which they point, and which appears to him
to be so much less visible in English towns of far greater
wealth and size. We do not expect in England to receive
learned studies in foreign literature from provincial colleges
or Universities. Till lately, indeed, such colleges have
scarcely been in existence. But the last twenty years have
made a great change in that respect ; a change which some
have feared must be chiefly external and nominal. The
doubt was raised whether we in England had enough raw
material for the making of many Universities, whether the
new ones would not lower the dignity of the name, by failing
to impress themselves on the respect of the country, by
inferior professors, by empty lecture-rooms, or, worst of all,
by succumbing to the infection of the merely utilitarian
standard around them. So far these fears have happily
proved groundless, though they may provide reason for
caution against proceeding too fast. But nothing can give
better hopes of the work such Universities are capable of
doing than the publication of such a book as this by Professor
Vaughan. It is not the product of his private leisure ; it is

[1] *Types of Tragic Drama.* By C. E. Vaughan, Professor of English
Literature in the University of Leeds. Macmillan.

a specimen of his public and official work. No greater proof could be given of the vitality of this particular University, at any rate, than that it provides a professor fit to deliver, and an audience fit to receive, such lectures as these. The great issues they raise, the wide field they cover, are enough to show that the University of Leeds can rise superior to the special temptation of the age in which it was born. There is no narrow specialism here. The range of study Mr. Vaughan imposes on his class-room recalls the stories of Dr. Hawtrey expecting Eton boys to be able to illustrate their Virgil from the great poets of Italy and France. Mr. Vaughan takes his pupils through almost all the whole history of tragedy, the great Greeks, Seneca, Racine, Alfieri, Shakespeare, Calderon, Goethe, Schiller, and Victor Hugo, with a final lecture on Browning, Maeterlinck, and Ibsen. It is quite possible, of course, to disagree with some of his opinions. What is not possible is to doubt that such a course of lectures, securely built on real knowledge, and full of the life which only a love of literature and faith in its serious value for humanity can give, must have inspired in some of its hearers an enthusiasm for these things which will last their lives.

The tragic drama is, in one respect, rather a melancholy subject to handle to-day. The most obstinate of optimists could not persuade himself that the theatre, especially the tragic theatre, is at this moment playing the part in the intellectual and moral life of Europe which it might play and has played in the past. It is true that there are names of some real distinction, two or three Germans, one Italian, and perhaps one Englishman, who will occur to every one as having done something to redeem the poverty of the theatre in the last and present generation, and, in consequence, as having had a right to share some part of Mr. Vaughan's last lecture with Ibsen and Maeterlinck. But they are not enough, either in number or in importance, to affect the general truth, that neither the higher emotion nor the higher imagination of the present day finds its way to the theatre. Dignity, greatness of mind and matter, that ancient σπουδαιότης which Matthew Arnold used to translate as 'high seriousness', exist among us still, but it is not our dramatists to whom we owe them. That is the contrast. It was precisely from their dramatists that the Greeks of the great age, the French of the seventeenth century, the English Elizabethans, the Germans of a hundred years ago, did get these great things. Everywhere, even in England, and till quite lately, the theatre was in close relations to the best literature of the day. Johnson, for instance, from age, deafness, and lack of inclination, did not often go to the theatre. But it would have been impossible for Boswell to keep the drama out of his biography. It is not an accident, but the natural and inevitable result of the relations then existing between letters and the theatre, that the life of the dictator of literature is full of such names as Goldsmith and Sheridan, Garrick and Mrs. Siddons. No such thing would be necessary to-day. We go to the play to be amused, or to be excited, not to satisfy any hunger of imagination, any thirst for poetry, in our nature. There are still tears in the theatre, as there is still laughter; but tragedy is no more to be measured by tears than comedy by laughter. Indeed, as Mr. Vaughan points out in speaking of Euripides, the greatest tragedy calls for a sterner note than that of pathos. 'Nothing is here for tears'; that, as he says, is the unspoken feeling which the greatest creations of tragedy call out.

The truth is, perhaps, that the theatre is essentially a public place, and we are no longer capable of high emotions in public. In spite of much political talk about Collectivism, the world, in its higher life at any rate, grows more and more individualist. Neither religion, nor art, nor literature affords any longer a means of public expression of feelings held by the people as a whole. There is no more carrying of great religious pictures in a procession of joy, there is no more national pride in the adornment of the national citadel or sanctuary, there are no more national theatres in which the art, and the poetry, and the patriotism, and the religion of a nation find, as they found in the theatre of Dionysus, a common and public expression. The lovers of art love it with a love at least as ardent as any Greek or Roman, but, whether they keep the beloved objects in their own cabinets or give them to the public, they no longer expect the people to share their enthusiasm. The lovers of poetry read great poems alone in their studies. Of religion itself the truest part is become a secret thing of which men no longer speak easily. Our highest moments are now those of solitude, not those of society. In the company of our fellow-men we find that both they and we are shy of lifting the conversation above the level of the ordinary and obvious topics of business and pleasure. What place has the tragic drama, the great drama of the poetic imagination, in such a world as this? Its very essence is open expression of the deepest things in the human soul, even open representation of them visibly on a public stage. How is such a world, so secretive of its deepest self, to face this ordeal of publicity? It cannot; and the result is that though *l'homme moyen sensuel* is no more the whole of humanity now than he ever was, he is become the whole of that small part of humanity which is allowed to tread the boards of the modern stage.

It is difficult to avoid asking these painful questions after going through the long and splendid history of tragedy as Mr. Vaughan gives it to us. But he himself deals mainly in retrospect, and his final lecture on Ibsen and Maeterlinck is the least satisfactory in the book. It is impossible here to follow him in his minute analyses of the work and methods of the various dramatists with whom he deals. One may say, though, that the ever-increasing fame of Aeschylus, who has been so much longer coming to his own than other Greek poets, will not be diminished by anything said by

Mr. Vaughan. But perhaps the world of late has been still more occupied with Euripides; and there is nothing better in the book than the chapter on that strange denier of the gods who yet more than any one else crowded his stage with gods, that humanitarian Radical who hated democracy, that romantic born out of due time who was bent on securing the picturesque at any cost, especially at that of the stately traditions of the great style which preceded him. But all this will be less new to most readers than the interesting account of Alfieri, who appears as 'the last great representative of classical tragedy'. Probably few readers of Mr. Vaughan's book will even have opened Alfieri; one, at any rate, who had just, and only just, done so, has been sent back to him by Mr. Vaughan, and hopes he will never fail in that due measure of gratitude which Ben Jonson found so sadly wanting in a certain lawyer to whom he had rendered a still greater service. 'Why, I was the man that first made him relish Horace!' People who take an interest in the drama might easily spend their time worse than in reading Alfieri. 'His supreme greatness,' according to Mr. Vaughan,

lies in this: that, retaining the classical model in its most severe form, he gave to it an intensity of action and of passion, he breathed into his characters a fire and fury, he informed the whole with a dramatic subtlety and vividness, which were hardly to be supposed possible within these narrow limits. . . . The result is that in his greatest plays the characters are painted with such fullness and richness of colour, such subtle mastery of light and shade as is elsewhere to be found only in the looser structure of the romantic drama — we might almost say, only in the tragedies of Shakespeare.

This is very high praise, and perhaps does something less than justice both to Aeschylus and to Shakespeare. One would have supposed that Aeschylus had not left it to Alfieri to prove that 'the classical model' is capable of as much 'intensity of action and passion', and as much 'fire and fury' s, this side madness, the human mind can bear. And to

place Alfieri's subtlety of character-painting side by side
with Shakespeare's is to do no greater kindness to Alfieri
than is done to those Elizabethan dramatists who were not
named Shakespeare by that unwise sect of their admirers
who insist on speaking of Shakespeare as if he were only the
greatest of their company. The weakness of Mr. Vaughan
as a critic lies, perhaps, just there, that he is insufficiently
sensible of the vast gulf that separates three Greeks and one
Englishman from all the other dramatists who have ever
lived.

But he has done students of the drama a real service by
recalling attention to Alfieri. Whether we ultimately prefer
the classical or the romantic method in tragedy, no competent
critic will deny that the classical method has some very
important advantages. Unity is the essential quality of all
works of art, and, that being so, a method which makes unity
comparatively easy has an initial advantage over one that
makes it comparatively difficult. But the English critical
tradition has, for the last hundred years at any rate, been so
' romantically ' disposed and so apt to be dazzled by Shakespeare's strokes of genius that it has been a little blind to
the defects of his method. Still, not even Shakespearean
idolatry can blind any one who really faces the study of the
drama as a whole and from the beginning, to the fact that
the intense concentration of interest exhibited by ancient
and modern classical drama is, so far as it goes, a great
source of strength to that drama. Now, if we put the ancients
aside for the moment, there is no one who is more likely to
convince Englishmen of this than Alfieri. For good or for
evil Englishmen do not generally like Racine. His great
formal beauties escape them, and they do not recognize
humanity in a world which is never seen out of court
dress. In fact, they find him somewhat insipid, and they
will be slow to think *Britannicus*, for instance, so great a play
as Mr. Vaughan thinks it. It is not there that they will

learn to value the modern classical drama. But let them
try Alfieri. There is no fear of his being found insipid.
'Love plays a far less prominent part,' as Mr. Vaughan says,
'in his tragedies than in those of Racine.' 'The Courtly
atmosphere is swept away. . . . The language, so far from
being smooth, errs, if anything, on the side of abruptness, of
what Alfieri would have himself called "ferocity".' And yet
Racine himself has not a tenser concentration of interest.
Not a moment, not a word, is wasted. The action pursues
its rapid course without ever being turned aside, and the
dramatis personae never take their eyes off the central business of the play. This has, as we can all see, some disadvantages ; we should not know Hamlet as we do know him
if he had made no digressions from the business of avenging
his father. But the present point is that it also has advantages, and that no one really understands the art of drama
who has not perceived them. Take the two plays, *Agamem-*
none and *Oreste*, which deal with the old story of the
Aeschylean Trilogy ; is it not difficult to deny that they
absorb and possess the reader in a way that would be almost
impossible to the looser structure of the romantic drama,
except where reinforced by the genius of Shakespeare ? Nor
is this intense unity incompatible with subtlety of portraiture.
On the contrary, as Mr. Vaughan says, 'that subtlety is often
surprisingly great.' The character of Clytaemnestra, in
particular, torn between passion for Aegisthus on the one
hand, and honour, shame, and the love of her children on
the other, is nobly conceived and finely carried out. It was,
indeed, Voltaire, as Mr. Vaughan ought to have mentioned,
who first attempted that reading of character, and he may
have taken it, as Professor Jebb suggested, from a couple of
lines put into her mouth by Sophocles. But nothing can
deprive Alfieri of the glory of having given us one of the
most living of tragic figures. Nor can such things as the
chevaleresque absurdity of Orestes, Pylades, and Electra all

clamouring for the right of being the victim of Aegisthus
while Aegisthus looks on and hesitates till it is too late, nor
that other absurdity of Orestes ultimately killing Clytaemnestra by accident, and without discovering it, in the course
of killing Aegisthus, deprive the dramatist who devised the
scene between Clytaemnestra and Electra in the first play,
and those between Orestes and Pylades and Electra in the
second, of the name of one of the great masters of his art.
It is true that the classical form has its penalties as well as
its gains. Its very sanity and simplicity allow it no such
means of concealing incongruities as are afforded by the fine
frenzies of the romantic poet hurrying us from heaven to
earth and from earth to heaven. Fire enough it has room
for ; and fire enough Alfieri has ; the flame of passion, the
white heat of the tragic situation ; but it only burns true
when it is fed solely on the proper business of the drama.
And that, to do Alfieri justice, is what, in his case, it is commonly fed on. No dramatist ever kept more closely to his
text. The amazing impression of energy he makes in his
best scenes is made without the assistance of fine writing,
metaphors, or adornments of any kind. He truly is what he
called himself in the letter prefixed to his tragedies, *forte,
breve, caldo e tragico.*

What, then, is it which, in the presence of all these great
qualities, we still find wanting in Alfieri, and, indeed, in all
the modern classical drama ? Is it not, as Mr. Vaughan
argues in one of his best chapters, that lyric escape of the
human spirit, that brooding and reflecting self-revelation,
which the Greeks provided through their choral odes and
the Romantics by their soliloquies ? In these serried plots
of Racine and Alfieri the pressure of the business in hand
seems to have overbalanced the sense of the world as a whole,
and of the heights and depths of human existence, in a way
that makes the play seem unsatisfying and incomplete as a
picture of life. What would the *Agamemnon* be without its

great choruses? Not what it is, certainly. What would *Hamlet* or *Faust* be without the great soliloquies? If there is sometimes loss, how much gain there often is in the lyrics and lyrical dialogues with which the greater Romantics have sprinkled their plays! Alfieri argues in his letter against a lyric style in drama; and what he says has one obvious side of the truth in it. But is there not another? After all it is the very claim and essence of poetry that it is the only right and natural utterance of things that lie at the very heart of humanity; and if the drama leaves these things out, is it painting all the picture of life? Mr. Vaughan thinks that the whole movement of dramatic history has been from the external to the internal, from action to character, from visibility to intimacy, and that this movement is still in progress. That may, or may not, be so. There is Maeterlinck, no doubt; but can most of us feel as sure as Mr. Vaughan apparently does that we know the true soul of Ibsen's *Enemy of the People* as well as we know that of the *Antigone* of Sophocles? Or is it only that there is not so much to know? In any case, whether there be such a development as Mr. Vaughan thinks, or whether, as others might argue, this inwardness and intimacy are less an affair of date or method than of the genius of the dramatic poet, there can be no question of their importance. The whole of life is the province of the dramatist. Thought as well as action, the soul and the body, secrets and externals, poetry and prose, they are all his to take and to use, if he can. His problem is how to use as much of them as he may within the limits of time and the law of unity that are the necessary conditions of his art. The interest of a book like this of Mr. Vaughan's lies in watching the interchange of art and material, matter now stretching art beyond its capacities, art now compressing matter till the life is gone out of it, both engaged for ever, within the mind of the artist, in that eternal struggle which is life.

The end, we must have faith to say it, is not yet. Great as the past is, small as the present may appear, the ideal is always in the future. And the quest of it is in this, as in other matters, the eternal business and pleasure of humanity.

WORDSWORTH'S CREED [1]

THE publication of a critical study by Mr. Raleigh is a literary event. Yet Wordsworthians will perhaps be forgiven a little nervousness at the announcement of another full-length and full-dress portrait of their poet, even though the signature in the corner be one so reassuring as Walter Raleigh. Criticism, even in the best hands, is apt to be almost exclusively intellectual. The mind is set to work examining, analysing, distinguishing, and it can hardly avoid helping itself by abstract classifications and formal laws. Yet to do that is almost inevitably to miss the secret of Wordsworth. Not only did he care for none of these things; he actively disliked, disbelieved, defied them. He avowedly aimed at delivering a message which strained the capacities of language, and rejected those of mere logic with scorn. The simplest of men, and the most occupied with simple things, he is also the profoundest, the most daring, Platonist in English literature. There are quite definitely, in his creed, more things in heaven and earth than the mere intellect will ever find a way to take account of. And there lies the danger. For the critical intellect, delighted with the pleasure of its own play, is apt to fancy itself the measure of all things. It is like a traveller, returned from a hasty journey through some strange Eastern country, knowing his own cleverness and his own industry and knowing all they could teach him, not knowing how much there is they could not teach him. And so he writes his clever book, or delivers his brilliant lecture,

[1] *Wordsworth.* By Walter Raleigh. (Arnold.)

happy as a man who has guessed a conundrum ; and he has
all his categories ready to hand, into which some things he
has seen will fit nicely so that he can comfortably praise
them, and some will not fit at all, so that he can just as
comfortably condemn them.   And there is no fault to find
with him, except that he has taken sailing across the ocean
to be the same thing as sounding its depths.

This method has often been used in criticism.   The critic
yields to one of the many temptations that lie around him,
the linguistic, or the historical, or the moral, or the purely
intellectual, and he has his reward.   But that reward is not
the one thing needed for him and for us—initiation.   Most
of all is this true in the case of Wordsworth.   You may
approach a Buddhist in the spirit of Wall Street as profit-
ably as you will judge Wordsworth by merely literary and
historical considerations.   Wall Street will report quite
truthfully of an Indian mystic that his economic instincts
appear to be imperfectly developed.   And you may, in the
same way, report things equally true and equally important
about Wordsworth.   But you will not be one step further
on the true path.   Wordsworth is a prophet and a seer or
he is nothing.   Cleverness will make little of him, beyond
an added reputation for cleverness.   He is a mystic, and it
may almost be said that the only way to approach him is
the mystic's way of silence and self-surrender.   No one clings
more earnestly to fact than he ; but it is only the *pia et
humilis inquisitio veritatis* that will reveal the truth of which
his facts are the visible form.   One must go inside to understand ; ' he only knew the Flame who in it burned.'

Mr. Morley says somewhere that it is a good habit
before reading a book to ask oneself what one expects to
find in it.   The Socratic occupation of asking oneself questions is not one, perhaps, that can be expected to commend
itself to an unleisured generation.   But it has its uses
nevertheless.   And it may not have been amiss, for once,

to aim, first of all, at getting some idea of what a critical study of Wordsworth should and should not be, before going on to see what Mr. Raleigh's actually is. It has at any rate the advantage of trying the critic as Mr. Raleigh deserves to be tried, by the severest of tests. He comes well through the ordeal. His book makes no epoch in the appreciation of Wordsworth; the hour for that is past, and also, it may be, not yet come. Wordsworth, it is certain, will be a living voice so long as there are English ears to hear him; but the ears may grow unaccustomed to his accent, and he may again some day need a new interpreter. For the present, we are too near the illumination that came, in verse and prose, from Matthew Arnold to need any new light as yet; we are not even far enough away from Coleridge to have forgotten his original herald voice or find its message meaningless or outworn. There is no third place ready yet beside the discoverer and the re-discoverer. Mr. Raleigh comes too early. Our intellectual air is just now full of hints and questionings, which may be the first broken utterances, often seeming to babble unintelligibly like a child, of a new era in the history of man's knowledge of himself; or they may be only one more instance of the eternal fluttering at the bars which cage the winged human spirit, and will die away in weariness and silence like the rest. But if the words we now hear as strange phrases implying stranger doctrines ever become accepted and familiar, and the philosophy of the 'subliminal self' and 'suggestion' and 'possession' pass beyond the stage of hypothesis, it may well be that new light may be shed on Wordsworth; a new interpreter may be needed, and, when he has been found, new illumination may shine on the human mind and soul from the poet whose wisdom came to him from without, by waiting and in silence, who turned away from the energies of the intellect to teach

> That we can feed this mind of ours
> In a wise passiveness;

who proclaimed, with the conviction that is at the root of all faith in spirit,

> We feel that we are greater than we know.

But that great opportunity for a great Wordsworthian, if it ever should come, has not come yet. And he who could have seized it best, the great Wordsworthian who gave his last years to the forlorn hope, not forlorn in his eyes, of bridging over the gulf that lies between seen and unseen, embodied spirit and disembodied—it is sad to think that he who, whatever opportunity there may be, would have been its best interpreter, will not be here to use it. Meanwhile, Mr. Raleigh does excellently what can be done to-day. He gives us a book which is systematic, and yet full of the sympathy which is so much more than system. He tells us all that is to be told, with admirable order and lucidity, and yet is quite conscious that the essence of Wordsworth is a secret, not to be explained but felt with the certainty that belongs only to the unprovable things—to faith, to love, to beauty. He has chapters on the obvious topics—the poet's childhood, the Revolution, Coleridge, poetic diction, nature, humanity, illumination—and has true, interesting, and often brilliant things to say about them all. He wastes no time in crossing swords with Wordsworth's detractors. The only passage at arms he has thought worth while to have is with a friend, himself a captain in the Wordsworthian army. Mr. Morley once allowed himself to say, in his brilliant introduction to a one-volume edition of the poet, that when Wordsworth 'tells us that

> One impulse from a vernal wood
> May teach you more of man,
> Of moral evil and of good,
> Than all the sages can,

such a proposition cannot be seriously taken as 'more than a half-playful sally for the benefit of some too bookish friend. No impulse from a vernal wood can teach us anything at all of moral evil and of good.' It is certainly little less than amazing that such a passage as this can occur in the course of a long and sympathetic essay on Wordsworth. And it is equally extraordinary that a critic so acute as Mr. Morley should not see that he has removed what is, as Mr. Raleigh most justly says, ' the very corner-stone of Wordsworth's poetry, and no less.' Without it he may or may not be a pretty poet, but his place as seer and teacher, as one of the greatest landmarks in the history of the human spirit, is entirely gone. For it is this particular thing which he spent his life in saying, and if it is false he is a false prophet, and there is no more to be said. To quote Mr. Raleigh, ' Might, wisdom, joy, peace, these were ' for Wordsworth ' not qualities projected by the imagination of man into a lifeless universe, but qualities that exist outside of man, and may pass into his life, if only he will be quiet and will attend.' He goes on to overwhelm Mr. Morley with a wealth of illustration from the poems; and it would be easy to add to his store, for the truth is that the whole of Wordsworth may be called one continuous assertion of this faith. To say with Mr. Morley that

> Through primrose tufts, in that green bower,
> The periwinkle trailed its wreaths;
> And 'tis my faith that every flower
> Enjoys the air it breathes

is a 'charming poetic fancy and no more', and to imply that the poet himself hardly thought it more, is really to stultify any number of eloquent pages in praise of Wordsworth.[1]

[1] Since this essay appeared Science itself has shown signs of adopting views very much nearer the Wordsworthian position than any one would have thought possible when the stanza quoted was written. See Mr. Francis Darwin's Presidential Address to the British Association, 1908,

This faith in the mystery of life that lies all round us, in the voices that the spirit may hear if it will but learn how to listen aright, is of the essence of Wordsworth, and to try to explain it away is to put oneself out of court as his interpreter. The truth he enjoyed and lived by seemed to him, in Mr. Raleigh's words, 'not to be attained by any sort of intellectual elaboration, but by a purging of the eye, an intense and rare simplicity of outlook. He was haunted by a sense that the truth was there, directly before him, filling the whole compass of the universe; the greatest and most obvious and clearest of all things, if only the eye could learn to see it.' And, if we ask him how the lesson is learnt, the poet's account of the way to attain the poetic vision is really not very far away from the saint's key to the beatific vision:—'If thou wert good and pure within, then wouldest thou see all things without hindrance.'

The only criticism that can be made upon Mr. Raleigh's treatment of this part of his subject is that he hardly brings out clearly enough the distinction between the two parts of the great Wordsworthian revolution. What is it that Wordsworth actually achieved? First, he proclaimed that poetry was in possession of but half her kingdom, and that he was come to put her in possession of the whole. She had had the hero; he would give her the peasant. She had had the rose; he would give her the daisy. 'The human mind,' as he said, 'is capable of being excited without the application of gross and violent stimulants; and he must have a very faint perception of its beauty and dignity who does not know this, and who does not further

in which the following sentence occurs:—'It is impossible to know whether or not plants are conscious; but it is consistent with the doctrine of continuity that in all living things there is something psychic, and if we accept this point of view we must believe that in plants there exists a faint copy of what we know as consciousness in ourselves.'

know, that one being is elevated above another in proportion as he possesses this capability.' He set himself to feed this faculty, of which he speaks, as it had never been fed before ; his special desire, as a poet, was to show that in the very commonest sight, in the simplest nature, in the *Small Celandine*, in *Simon Lee*, in *Poor Susan*, in a cloud or a daffodil, there is something of interest, of stimulus, of emotional inspiration, if one will but learn to look for it. And thousands of people have learnt that this is so since they have had him to teach them. He has transformed every hedgerow for them. They owe him a sense of sympathy and companionship in the barest of country lanes, with the help of which they can never be unhappy, never alone. They have tried his promise, and found it not to fail, but to be what it was to John Stuart Mill, the secret of a 'source of inward joy in which all human beings may share'. It is quite true that there were peasants, hedgerows, and flowers in literature before Wordsworth came. It is even true that there is more of the magic of poetry in Shakespeare's ' daffodils that come before the swallow dares ' than in all the flowers of Wordsworth ; but Wordsworth's daffodils, 'tossing their heads in sprightly dance,' and the use he made of them, have perhaps opened more blind eyes to the beauty of roadside flowers than the whole work of Shakespeare. Peasants and flowers were, after all, only pawns in Shakespeare's mighty game. They are Wordsworth's chief actors, through whose mouths he says what he most wants to say. And as for such poets as Cowper and Burns, who come nearer to Wordsworth's position, the one had not the force or breadth to anticipate his work and the other was entirely wanting in the clear-sighted coherence of will and understanding, so indispensable to the makers of revolutions, and so conspicuous in Wordsworth. So it was left for Wordsworth to accomplish alone his great achievement, that of showing that ' Paradise and groves Elysian', as he says, are not 'a history only of departed things', but also 'A simple produce of the common day'.

This is the first part of his work. And note that the unique sensitiveness to Nature which enabled him to do it was in him from the first. Mr. Raleigh, indeed, talks strangely of there being 'nothing Wordsworthian, so to say, about the boy Wordsworth', and of the 'ordinary vague stuff of human nature' out of which the poet was moulded. It is the one serious mistake in his book. Does he think that ordinary, un-Wordsworthian schoolboys find themselves often overcome, as the poet says he was, by 'such a holy calm' that

> bodily eyes
> Were utterly forgotten, and what I saw
> Appeared like something in myself, a dream,
> A prospect in the mind?

Is it his experience that the brains of most boys 'Work with a dim and undetermined sense Of unknown modes of being'? There is no need to multiply proofs; the 'unique things he brought from the mountains', as FitzGerald called them, were in Wordsworth from the beginning. And he very soon began to make his unique use of them. First there was this 'consecration of the commonplace' of which we have just been speaking, and in virtue of which he has been well called 'the most joy-bringing of English poets'. But that is not all; there is the other half of his special creed and work. He tells us in the second book of the *Prelude* how very early he became conscious of 'affinities In objects where no brotherhood exists To passive minds'; and offers as at least a possible explanation of what he felt that, when he seemed to be transferring his own enjoyments to inorganic natures, he was in reality conversing 'with things that really are', through 'the power of truth' coming in revelation upon him. And all through his life he believed that truth reached him in this way by 'quick and eager visitings' which, like those that came to his Highland girl, lay often beyond the reach of utterance, but were not the less real or beautiful for that. And out of them grew his doctrine, which Mr. Morley finds foolishness, the doctrine that Nature is not only a giver of joy, but a teacher of good. His wide imagination, which refused, as Mr. Raleigh says, 'to recognize the arbitrary boundary set between Nature and Man, sought for correspondences everywhere. All that he had seen in what is called the known world had been revealed to him by his emotions, by admiration, and fear, and hope, and love. In these emotions he found the secret and spring of man's life. When, therefore, they arose mysteriously in the mind he was not prepared to call them idle and unmeaning because no rational cause, as the phrase goes, was assignable to them.' It would be hard to find anywhere a better piece of critical work than this whole passage in which Mr. Raleigh makes plain the distinction between the earlier poets who were for ever finding emblems or symbolic meanings in nature, and Wordsworth who has in his mind no fanciful play of parallels, but 'a deep imaginative sense of unity in things, of real correspondences and connexions working through the universe of perception and thought'. In that faith he could cry out :—

> Love, now an universal birth,
> From heart to heart is stealing,
> From earth to man, from man to earth ;
> —It is the hour of feeling.

In that faith he, less like Rousseau than any man who ever lived, could take up Rousseau's rhetorical gospel of the life according to Nature and give it body and truth. In that faith he could assert that the abiding though unnoticed presence of fair sights seen long before may have

> No trivial influence
> On that best portion of a good man's life,
> His little, nameless, unremembered acts
> Of kindness and of love.

And in that faith he can even declare that what is best and most beautiful in his Lucy may be thought of as Nature's own work.   He never put his central doctrine of the formative and corrective influence Nature may have on all of us who will make the needful self-surrender with greater force or beauty than in the stanzas in which he utters this declaration :—

> Myself will to my darling be
> Both law and impulse; and with me
> The girl, in rock and plain,
> In earth and heaven, in glade and bower,
> Shall feel an overseeing power
> To kindle or restrain.
>
> She shall be sportive as the Fawn
> That, wild with glee, across the lawn
> Or up the mountain springs;
> And hers shall be the breathing balm,
> And hers the silence and the calm
> Of mute insensate things.
>
> The floating Clouds their state shall lend
> To her; for her the willow bend;
> Nor shall she fail to see
> Even in the motions of the Storm
> Grace that shall mould the maiden's form
> By silent sympathy.

The poetry of Wordsworth may be greater than his creed, and may be independent of it; but at least there should be no doubt that this is what the creed was, and that he, and he alone, was its discoverer.

SCOTT'S POETRY

THIS is a year of centenaries, and it has too many of the legitimate and inevitable order to admit the introduction of any that can be accused of being fictitious or arbitrary. This is not the centenary of Scott. That great honour must be disputed between a year long past, 1871, and a year which many of us will not live to see, 1932. But, without any actual centenary pretences, there is a reason why 1909 sends us back to the poetry of Scott. Readers of this journal are trained to be always looking back a hundred years. The year 1809 was the central year of Scott's poetic fame. It began with *The Lay* in 1805, reached its height with the publication and astonishing popularity of *Marmion* in 1808 and 1809, and began to pale in 1812 before the star of Byron, which rose with *Childe Harold* in that year. During the seven years between 1805 and 1812 Scott was the visible monarch of English poetry. His title might be disputed in public by the lingering conservatism of critics trained in the school of the eighteenth century, and in private by the faith and insight of the few friends and readers who knew what Wordsworth was, and what he must before long be known to be. But with the general mass of people who read poetry, Scott ruled as unquestioned king. He had sounded the note for which his world had been all unconsciously waiting, and he had his immediate, splendid, and well-earned reward.

That was pre-eminently the case in 1809, during which year purchasers were found for six thousand expensive quarto copies of *Marmion*. But few poets have lost their thrones so rapidly as Scott; and he has never been restored.

When Byron, the immediate supplanter, fell, it was not before a restoration of Scott. The crown of poetic popularity was put into commission, and what he had once enjoyed alone Scott had to divide not only with Byron but with at least half a dozen others, with Crabbe and Moore, with Wordsworth and Coleridge, with Keats and Shelley. So it continued till the beginning of the long and undisputed reign of Tennyson, which lasted down to our own day. All these poets taught their readers to demand some things which Scott could not give. The result has been that he has never recovered, and never can recover, the position he held in the years between Trafalgar and Waterloo. Perhaps a part of the explanation, too, lies in himself. The royal exile who finds another kingdom is the less likely to recover his own. The disputed claims of the poet were forgotten in the acknowledged sovereignty of the author of the Waverley Novels. And so it continues to the present day. Is there not some resulting injustice to the author of *Marmion*? The novelist is greater, no doubt, than the poet, but is the poet quite so negligible as he is commonly thought to be? Is there no room for the suggestion that 'back to Scott' must be one of the mottoes of an attempt to take a complete view of English poetry?

It is the business of poetry, after all, to take the whole of life for its province. If that be so, Scott did a part of its work which no one before him had attempted, and no one since has so well performed. He found English poetry divided between satire and meditation; Dryden, Pope, and Crabbe, we may say, standing on one side, Gray and Collins, Thomson and Cowper on the other. Besides these there was, of course, Milton; but he, then as always, is a figure apart, of no man's company, inevitably filling all with the sense of a great presence amongst them, but forming no school, so that the poets who most honoured and imitated him, such as Cowper and Thomson, have no real affinity

with him. If we put Milton aside, then, the poetry read
at that time was confined to these two schools, the school of
lyric and elegiac meditation, and the school of the study
of manners, of the criticism of life, especially that part of
life which is lived by rich people in towns. But lyrics,
elegiacs, and satires no more make the whole of poetry
than introspection and observation make the whole of life.
There remains what used to be thought the greatest of all
things, and the fittest for poetry : there remains action.
And part of action is physical action, a thing utterly
excluded from English poetry from the days of Shakespeare
to those of Scott. Most completely was it ignored in the
eighteenth century, when poets addressed themselves almost
solely to an intellectual class, living a town life spent in
talking, reading, writing, and society, divorced from all
kinds of bodily activity. The inevitable result is that their
poetry may enrich or amuse the mind, may delight the ear,
may console the heart; but it can never make the blood
run faster. It is sedentary poetry, composed by those who
sit and write for those who sit and read. And this remains
true to the very end, even after Cowper had changed so
much else in the atmosphere of his century. Indeed it is
true of that much greater innovator, Wordsworth, who
had begun his innovations some years before *The Lay of
the Last Minstrel* astonished the world in 1805. With him
as with all the rest, poetry remained a meditation on man,
on nature, and on human life. Into that world Scott broke
suddenly with *The Lay* and with *Marmion.* And in a
moment all the blood in the English world ran faster.
Poetry leapt at one bound out of the silence of the scholar's
closet, and out of the secrecy of the lonely walk, to mount
the soldier's saddle, to climb the hill with the sportsman,
to run races in the wind with the schoolboy. The new poet's
triumph was visible and instantaneous; was it ephemeral?
Can a glory be ephemeral which came of a gift of new

life to thousands who had never till then realized that
poetry had such gifts to give, or that their own lives had
any poetry in them? Can that be an ephemeral power of
poetry to which brave men, in the moment of danger, in
the very presence of death, went for an inspiring draught of
courage and endurance and hope? Has any poet, except
Euripides and Gray, ever received so great and moving
a testimony to his power over the heart of plain men as
is to be found in Lockhart's story of the scene at Torres
Vedras?

In the course of the day when *The Lady of the Lake*
first reached Sir Adam Fergusson, he was posted with his
company on a point of ground exposed to the enemy's
artillery; somewhere no doubt on the lines of Torres
Vedras. The men were ordered to lie prostrate on the
ground; while they kept that attitude the captain, kneeling
at their head, read aloud the description of the battle in
Canto VI, and the listening soldiers only interrupted him
by a joyous huzza whenever the French shot struck the
bank close above them.

Poetry that can play this part is not poetry that can be
forgotten. 'Deep in the general heart of men its power
survives'; it is secure, not of the highest place perhaps,
but of a place it can never lose.

That was the first achievement of Scott. He recalled
poetry to action, and men of action to poetry. And this
not only by his subject, but by his manner, his incomparable
lucidity, simplicity, and ease. Pope and Crabbe are often
difficult to construe; Gray and Collins are often difficult
to understand. But the plainest man in the world never
stumbled at one of Scott's sentences, never found his thought
or language obscure. That is a limitation, of course, on one
side. It is the weakness of Scott that he hardly appeals
to the intellect at all. People who think, and who find
thinking at once a necessity, a duty, and a pleasure, are
impatient of the easy-going thoughtlessness of Scott. Much

of his poetry seems to suggest that its author saw nothing
in all the world but a pageant, a double pageant of the
external world and of the life of man. It is as if he merely
saw it and never cared to think about it, to go below the
surface of it, to seek out its interpretation. One knows the
note :—

> The breeze, which swept away the smoke,
>   Round Norham Castle rolled,
> When all the loud artillery spoke
> With lightning-flash and thunder-stroke,
>   As Marmion left the Hold.
> It curl'd not Tweed alone, that breeze,
> For, far upon Northumbrian seas,
>   It freshly blew, and strong,
> Where from high Whitby's cloister'd pile
> Bound to St. Cuthbert's Holy Isle
>   It bore a bark along.
> Upon the gale she stoop'd her side
> And bounded o'er the swelling tide
>   As she were dancing home;
> The merry seamen laugh'd to see
> Their gallant ship so lustily
>   Furrow the green sea-foam.

It is a poetry that uses its eyes but not its mind. It
asks no questions and belongs very emphatically to the age
before responsibility for the universe was invented. It is
an external poetry, enjoying its own motion, dancing with
youth and joy and the open air and the animal pleasure of
being alive. Obviously it loses much by being only that;
but after all it is fair to remember how much it gains by
being that. Here is a poetry which is not doggerel, and
which yet sticks in the memory of a schoolboy, a boatman,
or a private of the Guards, as nothing else but doggerel
would. Here is the language of a scholar and a gentleman,
the eye of a poet, the ear of no mean master of the art of
metre, and the result is what a soldier can march to and
a child understand. That is no mean achievement; it is
what no one since Scott has achieved. Well might Scott

call himself one 'through whose head a regiment of horse had been exercising since he was five years old '. In all his most characteristic verse there is the sound and stir and colour of an army on the march. He said himself that his poetry had ' a hurried frankness of composition which pleased soldiers, sailors, and young people'. But, as Mr. R. H. Hutton pointed out when quoting that remark, it was not only young people. Scott's poetry is, he goes so far as to say, almost the only English poetry that runs easily in the heads of average men ; and he tells a story of an old man in a London street at night repeating to himself 'Charge, Chester, charge!' when a reply came out of the darkness 'On, Stanley, on,' and between them the two strangers finished the death of Marmion, took off their hats to each other, and parted laughing. And many people could bear their witness that when years begin to be felt and memory is not what it was, the one poet whose lines come back with the old certainty is Walter Scott, and particularly the author of *Marmion*.

Is that a gift that poets can afford to despise altogether? Has there not been loss as well as gain in the difficulty of the English poetry of the last hundred years? Poetry, once the dangerous fascinator of youths and maidens, the tempter whose magical delights were the terror of grave parents, has now for evil and for good become a thing which only grave people touch. The boys and girls who steal from the learning made easy of modern school-books to spend their time with Shelley or Wordsworth or Tennyson are not likely to fall victims to the vices of the Idle Apprentice. They are much more likely to give trouble by taking life too seriously. And, meanwhile, the rest are left out. The high intellectualism of all the poets since Scott has built a fence of difficulties round the garden of the Muses which only the nimble-witted can overleap. It is true that for those that are born nimble, or make themselves nimble by long and severe training, the fruits that the garden has to offer are richer, more varied, fuller of strength and meat, than the old. But for the others? Is there no reason to regret this old poetry of the plain man, which he who ran could read, the poetry that was at once understood and liked by 'soldiers and sailors and young people'?

There is another part of Scott's poetic achievement which has had a more permanent influence than either his simplicity or his return to action. It was he more than any one else in this country who carried English poetry out of the drab generalities of the eighteenth century into the colour and detail of the nineteenth. What Victor Hugo did for France Scott, followed by Byron, did for England. They made the abstract concrete. Man, the abstraction, found new life in actual and dissimilar men, courage was seen in the deeds of the brave, virtue was loved in virtuous men, and Nature herself came out of her philosophical sublimity of distance to be known at close quarters in the form of the Scotch hills and streams, the actual trees and flowers that had been the close companions of the poet's life. Of course Wordsworth did this in a greater way, and gave the nearness while adding to the sublimity. But Scott, who could not give the mystery of nature any more than that of life, gave its picturesqueness, the visible beauty and historical suggestion of it, in a way that appealed to a far wider public than Wordsworth knew how to reach. He was in fact the captain of the company of Romance. The work of the Romantics has all been a little vulgarized in process of time by its very success. As we look back now at Scott creating for us the historical feeling, and opening our eyes to the beauty of the wild hills and moors which scarcely any one before him had cared about, we not only find his sense of nature a little limited and his sense of history a little false; there is something worse than that. It is that at the end of the road on which he started us we see the Cook's excursionist with his crowd and noise, his bogus history, and his simulated enthusiasm for the picturesque. But, even there, in the very midst of the ugly sound and fury of the cheap wagonette, there is often a quiet eye or two which really sees and is genuine in the pleasure of its seeing. And, after all, drawbacks of this sort follow in the wake of most great movements. When all have got the tune it is useless to expect that only the judicious whistler should whistle it.

There is one other thing. Scott is one of the greatest of the poets of patriotism. No man of letters did so much as he did to fill Scotland and England with eager consciousness of the national life, pride in remembering its glorious past, courage and will in defending the great inheritance, faith in the future to which it must be handed on. It is true that all this was no discovery of his. The eighteenth century had no lack of patriotic poets. The age of Chatham could hardly be without them, and the national spirit will not forget the debt it owes to the poet of *Rule, Britannia,* or to the poet of the *Loss of the Royal George.* Nor has it failed since Scott's day. The Victorian age has made no mean contribution to the already splendid store. Many a strong man has felt his eyes grow dim, as they passed over the pages that contain *The Revenge,* or the great Wellington Ode, or *The Charge of the Light Brigade,* or a dozen other things by the same poet, or by others who loved England with a love as unquenchable as his, and in particular by Browning and Swinburne. Most of these poems strike a deeper note than Scott had it in him to strike. Still less could he reach the heights attained in his own day by the greatest of his friends in certain sonnets dedicated to National Independence and Liberty. The thing that Wordsworth would have died for was the spiritual greatness of England, a thing of which Scott knew little. What Scott cared for was her historic glories,

the visible place among the nations of the England of
Henry V and Elizabeth and Chatham, of the England that
never bowed the knee to Philip or to Louis or to Napoleon.
He was the very voice of what was greatest in the great
aristocracy which carried England through the long years
of war that filled his middle life.   He was the voice of the
thing which was the need of the moment, the thing that
has always come best from aristocracies, the voice of un-
questioning, uninquiring, unalterable will.   And he put it
into language which both the intellectual who gave the
commands, and the unintellectual who obeyed them, could
understand.   That was his great service.   Such a thing as

> Breathes there the man with soul so dead,
> Who never to himself hath said,
>   This is my own, my native land!

was poetry alike for palace, and camp, and cottage, and in
each for England.   Where could the schoolboy go better
for the fighting spirit which is the raw material of victory
than to the battle-pieces of Scott?

> They close, in clouds of smoke and dust,
> With sword-sway and with lance's thrust,
>   And such a yell was there,
> Of sudden and portentous birth,
> As if men fought upon the earth,
>   And fiends in upper air;
> O! life and death were in the shout,
> Recoil and rally, charge and rout,
>   And triumph and despair.

Perhaps criticism may fairly point to blemishes of detail
in this, but the look in the boy's eyes is the poet's sufficient
answer.   Scott cannot give us the great figures of the *Iliad*,
cannot rise to its height and greatness of action and
character, but he can make us live its joy of battle over
again; and not ignobly.   Where shall the young soldier
find finer inspiration, a voice that at once fits his needs and
makes him listen, than in Scott's heroic outburst,

> Sound, sound the clarion, fill the fife,
>   To all the sensual world proclaim,
> One crowded hour of glorious life
>   Is worth an age without a name!

Every boy knows it, of course; and the fact that every boy
knows and remembers it is the proof that it rings absolutely
true. One can never escape repeating the reflection that
Scott's lameness, which gave us a great man of letters, may
have cost us a great captain and a hero. Not that the hero
really was lost, of course. His chance came, as it always
does sooner or later, and he could not well have met it
better facing death on any stricken field than he met
it facing his creditors in those last brave years at
Abbotsford.

So, then, let us go back, at least occasionally, to the poetry
of Scott. The taste that cannot find pleasure in *Marmion*
must have been corrupted in some literary hot-house. The
lover of poetry who thinks he has reached a stage when he
need not care for—

> Each one the holy vault doth hold,
>   But the sea holds lovely Rosabelle!

had better descend a step or two, if not begin his ascent
altogether afresh. The man who scorns such verses as
' On Ettrick Forest's mountains dun ' is unduly limiting the
field of poetry, which includes plain life and common
pleasures, as well as glory and rapture and romance. Scott
is perhaps the best loved of all great figures in our literature. But his poetry does not need to shelter itself behind
the prejudices of personal affection. To a catholic taste
there is enough and to spare of good food in it. Some will
rejoice especially in the swift narrative of the great tales,
in which he certainly has but one English rival. Some
will choose his spirited, graceful, tender lyrics, *Rosabelle*, or
Jock of Hazeldean, or the *Pibroch of Donuil Dhu*, or *Waken
Lords and Ladies Gay*, or *Lochinvar*, or *Bonnie Dundee*, or

that little masterpiece *Proud Maisie*. Others, and in this intensely political country they may be the longest lived of all, will turn with most affection to the noble Introduction to the first Canto of *Marmion*, and renew their delight in the exquisitely simple landscape with which it opens, the art with which the poet passes from nature to war and politics, the imperishable eloquence of the great tributes to Nelson, Pitt, and Fox. Never, perhaps, has any nation lost three such men within the space of a single year, and nobly did the national poet respond to the greatness of the call. The glory of England will have passed away if ever her sailors cease to be inspired by the thought of him to whom

> as to the burning levin,
> Short, bright, resistless course was given.

The people of this island will no longer be a nation of freemen if ever her statesmen can read without a throb of pride and envy the tribute to the mighty pair of whom Scott could say, in words that a hundred years have not convicted of extravagance,

> With more than mortal powers endow'd
> How high they soar'd above the crowd!
> Theirs was no common party race
> Jostling by dark intrigue for place;
> Like fabled Gods, their mighty war
> Shook realms and nations in its jar.—

And not only freedom and glory, but life itself will have left her if ever the successors of Pitt fail to hear the clarion call of duty in the noblest lament ever uttered over the grave of an English Prime Minister—

> Now is the stately column broke,
> The beacon-light is quench'd in smoke,
> The trumpet's silver sound is still
> The warder silent on the hill.

THE WAVERLEY NOVELS [1]

THE subjects set for University prizes, or accepted as fit themes for University honours, have led to the ultimate publication of much rubbish, some useful and creditable books, and at least one work of historical genius. This little volume, by a young Indian civilian who lost his life in the Dharmsala earthquake, belongs to the middle class. Nothing could be easier than to write rubbish about Scott, but Mr. Young's book is far from being rubbish. Nothing at this time of day could be more difficult than to say anything about Scott which would really place him in a new light; that would be the work of critical genius; and, whatever may be said of other sorts of genius, critical genius does not flower before the age of twenty-five, at which Mr. Young died. But he has given a fresh and useful telling of the old story; and lovers of the Waverley Novels are just the people to like their old stories retold, and not least this story of the man to whom they owe so many of their happiest hours. So we have it all here in Mr. Young's chapters: there is 'the making of a novelist', that curious preparation of blood and character and circumstances which made the novels possible; 'the romance from Walpole to Waverley' which gives us as good a picture as we know where to look for of the thing which then lay on drawing-room tables and which, taken up by Scott, turned as suddenly to gold in his hands as the old plays and chronicles did in the hands of Shakespeare; and the other chapters deal with 'the novelist at work', his tools and his methods, and their result. This is, of course, the

[1] *The Waverley Novels: An Appreciation.* By Charles Alexander Young. (MacLehose.)

most difficult part of the task. People who like pulling
their pleasures to pieces to see what they are made of must
do the work themselves if they mean to be quite satisfied
with the result. In any other hands the process commonly
ends in the losing of some parts that seemed certainly
present in the whole, or in the finding of some the presence
of which is neither expected nor desired. So, for instance,
some of those who hold Scott highest as a master of the
historical portrait will be a little surprised to learn from
Mr. Young that it is above all things the Queen Mary of
The Abbot which justifies their opinion; and, on the other
hand, some who can go back to the novels again and again
with a satisfaction that never fails will say that Scott's
'middling' wisdom, so well compounded of this world and
another, is a larger element in their permanently satisfying
quality than Mr. Young makes it, and deserves a fuller
place in any final analysis of their charm. In the heroics
Scott did not always succeed, no doubt; he is rather a man
of the plain than a man of the mountains. But, after all,
most people live altogether, and all live mainly, on the
plain. Heroics are great things, the greatest of all, and
belong to the greatest moments: all honour to those who
provide them, and to those who can fitly receive them. But
honour also to those who provide a serviceable wisdom of
every day which we can use in those common hours when
we are neither doing nor dreaming great things, but yet
wish to be living as men of sense and men of honour. Is
not the 'golden mediocrity' of Scott's criticism of life, so
often scorned by fools, a large part of the secret of his permanent hold on the world? The *Prometheus Vinctus* is
a greater achievement than the odes of Horace; but Horace
will always have more readers; and not only among fools.

However, the more or less, in questions of this sort, will
always be a matter of rather delicate adjustment; and no
one has any right to complain if Mr. Young's measure does

not produce exactly the same results as his own. In these
cases it is not agreement with every word of a book that is
its best praise. A better, and one that Mr. Young has fully
earned, is that we put it down when we come to the end
with a clearer understanding of its subject and a renewed
and reinvigorated pleasure. No one will read this book
without wishing to begin one of the great novels forthwith.
And that is the praise always preferred to all others by the
true critic, because he is also, and before all things, a true
lover of literature. Such Mr. Young evidently was. If we
may judge by this little book, his premature death cuts short
a career which had in it the promise of excellent work.
Meanwhile, it is no small achievement to have written a
book about Scott which, coming in as it must on the top of
a century of glory, has yet managed to touch it without
dulling its brightness.

What is the secret of that century of glory? It is easier
to be dissatisfied in this point or that with other people's
explanations than to find a satisfactory one of one's own.
And perhaps there is a preliminary question which has first
of all to be faced. Will Scott's glory last? Is it lasting at
this moment? Men whose first memories of books gather
round *Ivanhoe* and *The Talisman* tell us that they find
to their disgust that their sons will not read the Waverley
Novels. Are they sorrowfully to accept the view that the
books they found so delightful were passing fashions, faded
now with the fading of Gothic castles and romantic heroines,
their kindly garrulity supplanted by the naked brutalities of
realism, their broad and simple reading of human character
eclipsed by the twisted subtleties of problem plays and
psychological stories? Must fighting be brutal, and love be
sordid, and romance be crime if it is to provide material for
an art that can be acceptable to a taste undermined, as it
seems to old fogeys, by three-inch headlines, halfpenny
papers, and cheap magazines? Is it fatal nowadays to

a novel, that ancient breath of the scholar and the gentleman present everywhere in Scott, the suggestion of a book written in a good library, and carrying the scent of it on every page? Does the modern novelist's choice lie between mere barbarism on the one hand, and a forced intellectuality, whether spurious or real, on the other, and is Scott's temper of cultivated common sense become impossible, gone from this generation beyond recall?

Perhaps the first comment with which such questions may be met is that to ask them at all is to give undue importance to the opinions of our contemporary public-school boys, 'barbarized' as they are by the long athletic debauch from which they are only now beginning to recover. And the publishers' lists may after all be put in evidence against the schoolboys. Somebody, and a very numerous somebody, still reads Scott, or the publishers would not produce new editions of him every year. Put down as many copies as you please to the demands of the prize-giving schoolmaster or the present-giving aunt, the deduction will still be insignificant compared with the output; and it will remain a sound argument that in the long run books are not published unless they can be sold, nor sold unless they are read. Scott's kingdom is still one of wide extent as well as one of high and ancient renown, extending even into unlikely places, as they discover sometimes who have opportunities of knowing what books are asked for in the up-country districts of our Colonies. Still there is no doubt that the schoolboy's evidence does count for something, and that the kingdom is not so wide as it once was. Why is that?

There are some obvious reasons. There is at all times a host of people who are incapable by temperament of caring to read or see or do anything but the latest thing. Very often they do not really take any pleasure in that; in fact, they are not in the habit of choosing their pleasures or occupations at all; they simply take them from their neighbours in sheer laziness, or, at best, in the vanity of wishing to be up in the things that are being talked about. For their purposes the Academy is more than the National Gallery, Sargent than Titian, Strauss than Bach. For such people Scott was everything seventy or eighty years ago; he is nothing to them to-day, and never will be again. But he has also lost ground with more serious people. The human mind has done a good deal of work since the Waverley Novels were written. Much of it has been mining work, and it cannot be denied that, as a result of it, the foundations of some parts of the great fabric raised by Scott are less secure than they were. The age of chivalry is dead, and neither Burke's speeches nor Scott's novels can now stand quite where they stood before its death was actually registered and certified; and they inevitably suffer a little from the manner of its death; for the truth is that it died, in large measure, of being found out. The greatest of all advantages a novelist can have is that his readers should believe in his personages, and, if possible, admire them, even before they appear on his stage. But we no longer believe, as Scott's world believed, in the picturesque chivalry of Crusaders, and even Highlanders and pirates have had their lustre a little tarnished. Then, again, Scott's was an imaginative age, and ours, to our loss, is a critical one. Between us and him lies a century of fierce intellectual debate on nearly all great questions; on religious questions, for instance; and the best Protestant of us all can no longer feel satisfied with the controversial methods of *The Abbot*. These disputes are still with us, and still with our novelists; but they now demand and get a less superficial treatment than it lay in Scott's nature to give them. And the novel in the present day has assumed the place held by the theatre in the age of Shakespeare, and later by the poets, especially from the rise of Wordsworth to the death of Tennyson—the place of a court where the ultimate questions, which every generation puts in a new shape, can be frankly asked, and can receive an answer which, whether adequate or not, is at least free from the preoccupations and foregone conclusions of the pulpit. In this way Scott again loses. People who want a novel to give them a key to the riddle of life will not go for it to *Rob Roy* or *Redgauntlet*. Then there is the unlucky learning of a generation whose knowledge has altogether outgrown its mind. Everybody nowadays believes himself to possess an historical sense, and very often it seems to deprive its owner of any other. Our information has increased so much that we can no longer take Scott's mediaevalism literally as his first readers did ; and our minds have grown so little that we see no more than they did that in a work of imagination accuracy in details of language or costume is a matter of very little importance. Memory has for the moment killed mind, as it so often does ; and we are slow to see that the playwright or the novelist who can make his characters live can always afford to smile at the critic who discovers that they swear unborn oaths and quote authors who flourished centuries after their day. The mention of the theatre suggests one other point in which Scott suffers with modern readers. He had a great knowledge of the drama, and he boldly and successfully led the novelists into an invasion of its province, the world of action. But, as usual, the conqueror caught some of the manners of the conquered. The formal contrasts of the stage ; the long soliloquies, so believable when one sees a man thinking aloud, so much less convincing when one reads them in cold blood ; the general air of strut and pose, so essential to the life of the old drama ; the grandiloquence written to win the applause of the pit ; all these have left their traces in the Waverley Novels, and they do not help Scott with the modern reader who is for the most part a prosaic democrat in a hurry.

All these things are, indeed, against him to-day, but what

great and undying things are for him, to-day, and to-morrow, and for ever! What a large-hearted humanity there is in everything he wrote—what prodigal variety he has, what a sovereign sanity! He was not a great artist, except, indeed, by a kind of accident, that is, by the fact that genius, even where it cares least about such matters as method and style, cannot help often doing things perfectly, as it were in its own despite. But he was something more and higher even than a great artist; he was a human being who found men and women the most interesting things in the world, and never thought one beneath the notice of his watchful eye and listening ear. What does he say of himself in *The Fortunes of Nigel*? :—

For ourselves, we can assure the reader . . . that we never found ourselves in company with the stupidest of all possible companions in a post-chaise, or with the most arrant cumber-corner that ever occupied a place in the mail coach, without finding that in the course of our conversation with him we had some ideas suggested to us either grave or gay, or some information communicated to us which we should have regretted not to have learned.

There is the novelist ready-made in temperament and provided in advance with his raw material; and, for the rest, Scott's training as a story-teller began apparently as soon as he was in breeches, perhaps before. It is curious to note, as Mr. Young says, that even in those early days his only trouble with his tales was that he could not finish them. Probably part of the reason then, as later, was that the shepherd so enjoyed his road and had such a kindly affection for his sheep, that he was apt to let them also enjoy it rather too freely, so that when he came to the end of his journey they were often found to have strayed a little loosely, and the business of getting the flock together again became a somewhat hurried and difficult affair. And no doubt he is inclined to take them to rather unlikely places, because, except in *The Bride of Lammermoor*, he never can have the

heart to take them to the shambles. That is a defect, of
course ; sheep do, in fact, generally end by going to the
shambles, and human beings are at least so far like them
that they go there very often too.   And it is true that Scott
is open, like Wordsworth, to the charge of averting his eyes
' from half of human fate ' ; wide country as he covers, it
must be frankly admitted that he makes no approach to the
boundless universality of Shakespeare.   That rivalry his
good sense set aside at once—even in the hour when the
whole world was at his feet—with the well-known sentence
of plain-spoken contempt :—'The blockheads talk of my
being like Shakespeare ; not fit to tie his brogues.'   He
was safe enough, indeed, on that side ; taking himself too
seriously was the last fault likely to be committed by the
man whose one literary sin was that he would not take his
work quite seriously enough.   And, of course, the wisdom
of his modesty is plain enough now.   He has neither the
highest heights, nor the deepest depths, nor the infinite
range, of Shakespeare.   He is as incapable of the profundity
of Hamlet as he is of the poignant passion of the great
sonnets. It is fair to add that he is equally incapable of that
something of morbidness the presence of which in the sonnets
cannot be denied, and of that tendency to the display of
merely verbal or logical dexterity which in Shakespeare
sometimes betrays the professional man of letters.

But when all differences are admitted Scott is still the
one man who has a breath of the Shakespearean air about
him.   We come away from both with a feeling that the
world is a big place full of stir and business, full of life and
love and beauty.   We think of both as looking on at the
spectacle of it all with kindly eyes, and telling its tale with
something of the same air of prodigal and magnificent ease.
Both give us the impression of companionable men, who
are going a journey with their creations, and take pleasure
in being with them ; not, as so many modern novelists do,

of statisticians collecting dull facts, or anatomists dissect-
ing dead bodies for which we must be thankful if they are
not worse than dead. Yet Shakespeare and Scott are not
themselves lost in their characters. The limitations of the
dramatist do not, indeed, allow Shakespeare to reveal much
of himself, while Scott reveals a great deal. But there is a
likeness in their attitude to their creations. They know
and enjoy every inch of them, and have a kindly feeling
for their own children; but they do not lose their own
identity; they themselves stand aside, like nature herself,
as we used to conceive her--the kindly nurse, who loves
her children, and gives them a frequent hint of the way
they should go, but always ultimately lets them run alone,
and meet the destiny they make for themselves, even if it
be a broken head. Scott is, no doubt, weaker-hearted than
Shakespeare, and when it comes to the last moment his
good nature will not let him refuse to give his hero and
heroine the sort of ending that fairy godmothers provide.
But these are not the moments for which we remember
him—who would not give a good deal to get rid of the last
chapters of *The Heart of Midlothian*?—and elsewhere his
attitude is commonly that of the humorous reason which
sometimes seems to be the genius of the world. There, too,
he is once more the small Shakespeare. He loves as Shakespeare does, as life itself does, to mingle touches of humour
with his saddest pages. The smile that enters the room with
Caleb Balderstone is never far away from the most tragic
figure in all the novels; and the girl whose fate we watch
with more anxious and breathless interest than that of any
other heroine who has only prose to tell her story is shown
to us again and again with the Laird of Dumbiedikes at
her side. It is in the same spirit that the so heroic and
so unheroic immortalities of Hal and Falstaff are unfor-
gettably united. No man, in fact, has shown so much as
Scott of Shakespeare's combination of high and true romance

with a steady consciousness of the prosaic side of life, its common sense and common business, its humour, its reasonableness, its hard bottom of fact.

It is this breadth of sympathy which more than anything else makes Scott still the greatest novelist in the English, and perhaps in any, language. His business is not with some side-study of disease, or eccentricity, or crime; it is with the whole in which these things are seen to be the exceptions; and if he forgets either, as indeed he often does, it is the exception, and not the law, that is forgotten. He carries with him everywhere an air of Homeric largeness, of the largeness of life itself. How gladly, as Sainte-Beuve felt, one goes back to bathe oneself in his streams of purity, health, and freshness after any long spell of Balzac or, one may now add, of Balzac's degenerate successors! Other men and women have gifts that he has not; but no one combines so many as he. Flaubert thought him the only English novelist who possessed the sense of composition; but however that may be there can be no doubt of the extent and variety of his gifts. He has, for instance, the poetry which is not in Dickens, the swift energy which is not in Thackeray, the largeness both of matter and manner which is not in Jane Austen, the lightness of touch which is not in Charlotte Brontë, the fresh air and motion of life which are not in Balzac, the tenderness which is not in Dumas, the limpid ease which is not in George Eliot, the artlessness which is not in Stevenson, the quietness and simplicity which are not in Mr. Meredith. With whom else shall we compare him? He is not the cleverest, or the wittiest, or the profoundest of novelists; but none is so sure of immortality. For there flows in him the clear and stream-like suavity of life itself, and that is the one thing whose pleasure never fails as the generations and centuries go by.

KEATS[1]

No poet, it seems, is so much with us just now as Keats.
The year[2] is little more than three months old and already it
has given us the facsimile of the manuscript of *Hyperion*,
and these three editions of the poems. It is true that the
Chiswick Quarto Edition is a mere reprint of the text, and
that Mr. Thorn Drury's edition with the introduction by
Mr. Bridges has appeared before, and contains nothing in
its present shape that is not to be found in the original two
volumes of 1896. But the fact that publishers find it worth
while to issue and reissue so many editions of so great a
poet is one of good augury, not only for the ever-living
glory of Keats, but also for the future of the intellectual and
imaginative life of the English nation. And perhaps of
more than the English nation. Indeed, we have just been
told by a very distinguished French man of letters that we
English are not a nation at all, but only a race. That may
or may not be so. But, even if it were so, and we had no
common inheritance but that of blood and language, a race
that had created such a literature as ours, and carries that
literature with it wherever it goes, would be playing no
small part in moulding the mind of the humanity of the
future. And as the enterprises of the publishers are the
result of business considerations, we may assume that the
English race does carry its literature with it as it travels

[1] *The Poems of John Keats.* Edited with an Introduction and Notes
by E. de Sélincourt. Methuen. *The Poems of John Keats.* Edited by
G. Thorn Drury, with an Introduction by Robert Bridges. Two volumes.
The Muses' Library. Routledge. *The Poems of John Keats.* Two
volumes. Edited by George Sampson. The Chiswick Quarto Series. Bell.
[2] 1905.

along the ever-expanding road. And there is not a great
deal of it that is better carrying with us than John Keats.
The faults that all the world finds in us, the hardness of
disposition compounded in varying degrees of the Puritan
and the practical man, the tendency to take the British
Constitution as part of the eternal nature of things, the
inclination to pose and to preach, none of these things are
in Keats at all. He is the poet of beauty; of beauty in
nature, in the art of words, in human life and story. It is
true that his life is a progress from sensuousness to sympathy,
and that he came to the strongest conviction, as strong as
that which Tennyson put into *The Palace of Art*, that self-
absorbed abandonment to the aesthetic pleasures is a drinking of deadly poison, fatal to the highest possibilities that lie
before men, not merely as human beings, but as artists. But
though that doctrine is to be found in his poems, in *Sleep
and Poetry* for instance, and in *Hyperion*, it is not the pre-
vailing impression they leave behind them. Other men
might moralize beauty better than Keats; his business was
to realize its presence to a unique degree. This poet and
that in our history had gifts which he had not; greater
gifts than his, and his gifts in a greater degree; but none
had this gift in his peculiar measure—the gift of seeing
beauty everywhere, till the reader who travels through his
poems feels that the world, within and without, has become
an enchanted garden, the small is seen not as insignificance
but as delicacy, the large not as heaviness but as majesty,
action takes a new grace, and rest a new dignity, and even
the fierce fever of sorrow is drowned in the tide of sympathy
which it awakens. This is Keats's unique achievement;
and it is well that the publishers should keep it always
before us by their reprints, and that we should seize the
opportunities they give us to go back to a poet of whom
assuredly the world does not stand less in need as it gets
older.

The most important thing in the Muses' Library Edition is the introduction by Mr. Bridges. Mr. Bridges is not only a poet, but a profound student of the poetic art, and this thoughtful and suggestive essay is probably the best thing that has been written on the art of Keats. Every word of it has that note of personal experience which can only come to those who have themselves faced the difficulties that beset poets in their work. Whether it is the original conception of a poem that he is discussing, or the general lines of the design on which it is to be built up, or the details of expression and ornament, Mr. Bridges always gives us the impression of having been there himself, and of viewing the problem from the poet's point of view as well as the critic's. His introduction is, therefore, emphatically a thing to be read by every one who takes an intelligent interest in poetry. But it is a pity that he has not taken the opportunity of a reprint to revise it. One differs from such a critic with hesitation, and it is only after repeated re-examinations of the text and of his comment that we venture to assert that in more than one important place he has strangely misunderstood Keats. *Hyperion* is in some ways Keats's greatest performance, and Mr. Bridges has devoted proportionate attention to it. Most of what he says is admirable; but when he comes to discuss the reason why Keats gave the poem up, he seems to us to fall into a serious mistake. He writes that Keats himself declared the poem was given up on account of his dissatisfaction with its style; but he adds, one cannot read to the end without a conviction that the real hindrance lay deeper. . . . The first two books describe the conditions of the older gods and are impassioned with defeat, dismay, and collapse; the third introduces the new hierarchy, and we expect to find them radiant, confident, and irresistible; but there is no change in the colour of the poem; of the two deities introduced, Apollo is weeping and raving, and Mnemosyne, who has deserted the old dynasty for her hope in the new, 'wails morn and eventide.' It is plain that the story was strangling itself.

But look at the third book on which the question turns.
There are only 135 lines of it, but they are enough to show
that Mr. Bridges has missed the plan of the book. It is
quite true that Apollo is weeping. But why? Not because he
is a member of the new hierarchy, but because he is not. He
feels confined in Delos, and vaguely knows that there is
some greater place and destiny for him to fill.

> Are there not other regions than this isle?
> What are the stars? There is the sun, the sun!
> And the most patient brilliance of the moon!
> And stars by thousands! Point me out the way
> To any one particular beauteous star,
> And I will flit into it with my lyre,
> And make its silvery splendour pant with bliss.

And then, as the unspoken answer of Mnemosyne dawns
upon his mind, the new note begins to be heard—

> 　　　　　　　　　　　　　　'I can read
> A wondrous lesson in thy silent face:
> Knowledge enormous makes a god of me.
> Names, deeds, gray legends, dire events, rebellions,
> Majesties, sovran voices, agonies,
> Creations and destroyings, all at once
> Pour into the wide hollows of my brain,
> And deify me, as if some blithe wine
> Or bright elixir peerless I had drunk,
> And so become immortal.' Thus the God,
> While his enkindled eyes, with level glance
> Beneath his white soft temples, steadfast kept
> Trembling with light upon Mnemosyne.
> Soon wild commotions shook him, and made flush
> All the immortal fairness of his limbs;
> Most like the struggle at the gate of death,
> Or liker still to one who should take leave
> Of pale immortal death, and with a pang
> As hot as death's is chill, with fierce convulse
> Die into life; so young Apollo anguished:
> His very hair, his golden tresses famed,
> Kept undulation round his eager neck.
> During the pain Mnemosyne upheld
> Her arms as one who prophesied. At length
> Apollo shrieked; and lo! from all his limbs,
> Celestial—

So it ends, as we have it; though Woodhouse, whether with any authority from the poet or not, added in his copy the six significant final words

> glory dawned, he was a god.

But, indeed, they are not needed to prove the general drift of the argument. The story is not 'strangling itself' at all. It is being born again. The note of the passage is that of prophecy, of eager anticipation, of new birth, life, deity, immortality. The whole fragment is the transition from the old hierarchy to the new, and if it had been continued the young gods would no doubt have appeared as 'radiant, confident, and irresistible' as Mr. Bridges desires. But, in spite of this and one or two other curious defects, Mr. Bridges has rendered a great service to students of Keats by his introduction. His key to *Endymion*, for instance, even if that also be open to criticism in detail, will give many readers the courage they have hitherto lacked to force their way through that forest of tangled and pathless beauty.

The new edition by Mr. de Sélincourt carries the good fortune of the Keats student a stage further. It has its defects, no doubt. The book is too big. There are advantages in keeping to one volume, but they are bought too dearly when such a poet as Keats, who of all men demands an atmosphere of perfect ease, is put into a volume which the hands are reluctant to hold. Another odd fault in the book is that the notes give no references to the pages of the text, and, therefore, when one is reading a short poem it is very difficult to find the notes to it. These are practical defects which have their importance; but, in spite of them, Mr. de Sélincourt's has some claim to be considered the best edition of Keats in existence. Indeed, there are many points of view from which his one volume is to be preferred to Mr. Forman's two. He makes no pretence of rivalling Mr. Forman in his exhaustive record of textual variations; but he records an enormous number, all probably that are of

the slightest importance, far more than many readers will
care about.   But the main object of his work is neither the
establishment of the text of Keats nor the interpretation of
his thought.   It is the discussion of the sources of his inspiration.   His admirable and scholarly introduction, his notes,
a learned appendix 'on the sources of Keats's poetic vocabu-
lary', and a useful glossary of his language with references
to the earlier poets from whom he may have learnt it, all
unite to make the relation of Keats to his predecessors the
special feature of the book.   Mr. de Sélincourt has, of course,
the defects of his qualities.   One cannot be so learned without
paying the inevitable penalty.   People who remember everything themselves always fancy other people do the same,
and consequently always put down all poets as echoes of
their predecessors.   Tennyson complained that he was accused
of copying poets he had never read ; and Keats is assuredly
innocent of any conscious or unconscious reminiscence of a
great many of the passages quoted by Mr. de Sélincourt as
his originals.   It is absurd, for instance, to assume that when
Keats writes of Clymene sobbing 'among her tangled hair',
he is thinking of Milton's 'tangles of Neaera's hair', though
it is not quite so absurd as the further supposition that
Milton's line is a reminiscence of Peele's

> Here comes my lover tripping like a roe
> And brings my longings tangled in her hair.

Poets who write the same language cannot avoid sometimes
using the same words.   But, though there are too many of
these notes of superfluous and misleading learning, they are
only a small portion of the whole, and cannot seriously
detract from the value of Mr. de Sélincourt's work.   He has
done more than anybody else to exhibit the true relations
between Keats and his predecessors, great and small ; he has
slain the legend that Keats owed all he knew of classical
story to Lemprière, and he has shown that the influence of
Spenser on his style was less, and that of Wordsworth on his

mind and character more, than has been commonly thought.
This is good and useful work; and Mr. de Sélincourt will
have the gratitude of all students of English poetry for
doing it.

And yet, after all, what a little way such investigations
carry us! Literary analysis can no more give the secret of
genius than chemical analysis can give the secret of life.
Keats is Keats; a unique, original, indefinable thing; and
it takes more to make him than any clever compounding
together of Spenser and Milton and the rest will achieve.
It is the child, and not the schoolmaster, that is father of the
man. The first words Keats gave to the public had all
himself in them; it had not all come to fruit or even to
flower, but it was all there, needing development only, not
creation. From the beginning he lived and watched 'nature's
gentle doings' as no one else ever did. Watched—that was
his business; not interpreted—that was Wordsworth's. No
exquisite delicacy of detail escaped him. He was from the
first the prettiest poet there ever was, and only grew into
the most beautiful. To see things and feel them, to dream
and to be passive, that is the human experience that he
had to a unique degree. From first to last his home is in
quiet places; it is for him to write the ode to Autumn, not
the ode to the West Wind. And so with the other things
about him. The very first poem, in the first volume, 'I stood
tiptoe upon a little hill,' is full of the delight in the beauty
of words—

O Maker of sweet poets, dear delight
Of this fair world :

and in the beauty of Greek story,

So felt he, who first told how Psyche went
On the smooth wind to realms of wonderment;

and he has only to develop, not to change.

It is in these things that the essential Keats lies, the same
from first to last, not the greatest poetic force of the nine-

teenth century, but the most purely poetical. Shelley might conceivably have been an agitator or Wordsworth a clergyman. Keats could in no circumstances have been anything but a poet. His royal, almost Oriental, fertility of imagination transforms the world at his pleasure ; and if the selecting and rejecting gift of the artist had not had time for perfect growth in his brief twenty-five years, it still is the fact that his mind, in its weakness as well as in its strength, was essentially the mind of a poet. With the masterfulness of a whole-hearted and whole-minded personality he compels us to see the world *sub specie pulchritudinis* ; while we are with him his high doctrine is true, and beauty is truth for us, and truth beauty ; and even when we have left his presence, and other elements of truth have forced themselves upon us, the vision he revealed is still unforgotten, the impression made upon us ineradicable, and we have no choice but to believe that beauty if not the very fullness and presence of truth, is at least truth's authoritative witness and inspired prophet.

SHELLEY[1]

SHELLEY is the poet of youth. But the youth of which, in his inspired moments, he is the divinest voice that ever breathed in this world, is that which never grows old, the eternal youth which is the very essence and life-blood of the human spirit. It is, therefore, no confession of unfitness for his task which Mr. Clutton Brock makes when he says in the last words of this book, 'I have written about Shelley as a middle-aged man for other middle-aged men.' The poet of youth is something much more than the poet of the young. There is something of youth, as there is something of childhood, which remains to the very end in all who are really alive. To be merely middle-aged is to be dead. Youth, however immature, is beautiful in itself, without any of the gifts that can only come with time; but age, if it be merely itself, if it has dropped all the hopes and graces of youth, is a thing withered, hideous, and hateful. Shelley is the embodied voice of youth's eternal elements, of the youthfulness which age needs to its last hour, and beyond. It is true and obvious that he is also the voice of less immortal things, of youth's crudity, youth's passionate one-sidedness, youth's curious substitution of an abstract humanity for actual and individual men and women, youth's impatience and incoherence, its abstract and rationalizing absurdity. But we, or some of us, are middle-aged, and can and ought to do for Shelley some of the purging and selecting work which time and his own rapidly maturing mind were beginning to do

[1] *Shelley: The Man and the Poet.* By A. Clutton Brock. Methuen. *Shelley: An Essay.* By Adolphus Alfred Jack, Fellow of Peterhouse, Cambridge. Constable.

for him when they were interrupted by the catastrophe of
Viareggio.   Mr. Brock has not been afraid to take his part
boldly in that work.   But the essential and immortal Shelley
remains, the pure spirit who is as certainly the eternal poet
of youth's ardour and aspiration as Wordsworth is of man's
grave and tender-hearted wisdom.

Mr. Brock says that he wrote his book to please himself,
the best of all reasons for writing books.   Most good criticism
arises from the desire of analysing our own pleasures and
justifying our own judgements.   And if the pleasures and
judgements are those of a fine intellect, other people besides
the author will enjoy the analysis.   That is what happens
here.   There are no new facts in Mr. Brock's book, only
a new mind applied to the old facts.   He has no discoveries
of new poems to record, no new letters to print, no fresh
information to impart about Harriet, or Timothy Shelley,
or *The Necessity of Atheism*, or any of the other problems
and persons that made the crises of the life of Shelley.   He
enters into no competition with Professor Dowden, by whom,
as he generously says, 'the complete biography of Shelley
has been written once for all.'   His object has simply been
to give a representation of Shelley based, as far as possible,
upon his own letters and works and upon the writings of
those who knew him, and his desire has been neither to
defend nor to attack Shelley, but, as he himself puts it, to
' represent him as he was, and to say exactly what I think of
his character and poetry '.

The result is a book of which every page is honest and
interesting, and many are brilliant; probably the best study
of Shelley that has yet been written.   It is full of digressions,
as is the way of books that are alive.   And as few people have
a clearer understanding of the art of poetry than Mr. Brock,
the digressions on such subjects as the English lyric, art and
Puritanism, prose and poetry, and similar large questions,
are among the best and most stimulating things in it.

Mr. Brock is always travelling from the particular to the universal, and Shelley's life and writings lead up to statements of principle which may not always command assent, but never fail to provoke thought or to have a good deal to say for themselves. 'The experience of emotion is the chief end of existence' requires a context, no doubt, for its justification, but it is, at any rate, an interesting parallel to Ruskin's saying that the function of art is to provide noble grounds for the noble emotions. Again, it would not be easy to give the distinction between prose and poetry better than Mr. Brock's rule that 'when reason is subsidiary to emotion, verse is the right means of expression, and, when emotion to reason, prose'. Things of this sort abound in the book, and make it much more than a mere book about Shelley. As that, its defect is, perhaps, that it is a little too cool and collected. A good fault, no doubt, in this case, for it is only too easy to catch fire when one touches Shelley. But even middle-aged readers will feel that Mr. Brock is almost invariably unjust to Shelley's beautiful prose, and will find him decidedly grudging in his praise of some of the very finest of the poems, as, for instance, the *Stanzas written in Dejection*, the *Lines written among the Euganean Hills*, and, most of all, the *Hymn to Intellectual Beauty*. Still, he can praise unreservedly enough when he chooses; and few will lay down his book without a heightened sense of the wonderful powers of Shelley, who, as Mr. Brock says, even when he attempted the impossible, and therefore failed, managed to produce 'beauties beyond the reach of artists who attempt the possible'.

Of the man Shelley he writes with the same cool, discriminating, unblinded admiration. What he says will not please everybody; few books do which try to see the whole of a subject. The extreme devotees of Shelley, whose eyes never move from the fair face of their golden divinity, will be impatient with one who has been all round it and, having

seen that some less important parts of the idol are made
of inferior metal, has honestly reported that fact. The
Bohemians, who have sometimes impudently claimed the
severe and ascetic Shelley as belonging to their company,
will be still less pleased. For they will find the one thing
that attracts them to Shelley treated, as it should be treated,
by common sense and common conscience, and, as the inevitable result, admitted to be the one grave blot on a very
beautiful character. No character can be harder to write
about than that of Shelley. For unless we blind ourselves
one way or the other, we are face to face with the two
apparently incompatible facts that Shelley was among the
best, most unselfish, and most spiritual men who have ever
lived, and that on one great occasion and on several small
ones he behaved about as badly as a man can behave. That
is the difficulty, and it has to be met. Few people who care
about—what Shelley himself cared about so passionately—
the moral progress of mankind were quite satisfied with the
atmosphere of special pleading and partiality with which
Professor Dowden clouded the issue. Mr. Brock comes much
closer to the problem. It is probably true, as Mary Shelley
said after her husband's death, that Shelley never did anything which he did not honestly believe to be right. But
that does not carry us very far. It leaves us in the old
difficulty of the distorted conscience; probably Torquemada
and Philip II could say as much for themselves. The point
is how such a man as Shelley could come to think it right
to act as he did act.

The answer is probably twofold. In the first place, exceptional natures have exceptional weaknesses, as the lives
of the saints abundantly show. Especially at the beginning
of life heights are apt to involve depths. But that is not all.
It is not merely, as Mr. Brock says, that the reason why
most young men do not behave as foolishly or badly as Shelley
is that they have not his courage. Many a man who knows

that in a world where all secrets were revealed he would
not be fit to kneel at Shelley's feet, knows also that better
things than cowardice would have kept him from doing
some things that Shelley did. The real explanation of
Shelley's doings is not courage, but ignorance; ignorance
of himself, of other men and women, of human character
and human life. Many boys of sixteen know more of themselves and of the world than Shelley ever came to know
at all. Probably no document in the whole world shows
such an abysmal ignorance of human, and especially femi-
nine, nature as the famous letter to Harriet after his flight
with Mary. And that letter does not stand alone. The
truth is that the key to the weak things in his character is
the same as the key to the weak things in his poetry; it is
his isolation from the realities of human life. All idealists
are in danger of being ineffective because they are felt to be
inhuman, without pleasure in human life as we know it and
live it. Shelley, the most ideal of idealists, suffered worse
things than ineffectiveness from this cause. He took too
little interest in ordinary life ever to know anything about
it, and he fixed his eyes so exclusively on the ideal that he
was apt to clothe every woman he saw in it and think her
divine till the ideal garments came off, on which he at once
fancied her a daughter of hell, or, more exactly, in his own
language, applied to one who had been 'a sister of his soul'
not long before, 'an artful, superficial, ugly, hermaphroditical
beast of a woman.' There are some men, men of humour,
for instance, who fail because they have such a pleasure in
life as it is, and such amusement in the contemplation of its
incongruities that they can never really work at improving
anything. The real is for them so pleasantly and laughably
unlike the ideal that it would be a pity to do anything
to spoil the humour of the situation. Shelley was just the
opposite. He knew nothing of the real, and, as Mr. Brock
says:—

There was something insipid in what he admired even in real people, for he was not aware of their real qualities; and these, when they forced themselves upon his notice, affronted his dreams, and therefore seemed to him devilish instead of human.

It was so in the highest thing of all. His love was precarious, because, to quote Mr. Brock again, he never loved women for themselves, but for perfections he imagined in them, and 'unconscious desire which always went to his head disguised itself as a recognition of intellectual and moral perfections'. He was as ignorant as Rousseau of the moral weakness of man, and as ignorantly confident as Rousseau that vice, instead of being curbed by human institutions, was simply caused by them ; and, like most people who fancy that original sin is only a theological bogey, he was surprised and inconvenienced by running up against it, as was inevitable, a good many times in the course of his life. However, most of us are as far as it is possible to be from having the right to throw a stone at Shelley. We are not likely to make mistakes through being too much occupied with 'intellectual and moral perfections'. Still, the honest critic is bound to note the facts ; and the central fact about Shelley is that it was his isolated idealism, his refusal to see the ideal in the real, his conception of it as something far apart from actual life and imperfect human beings instead of something working in them, transforming them as well as transcending them, that was the cause of his unfortunate illusions and disillusions about a succession of women, and also the cause of his being the author of the most unreal and the most inhuman of all the great poems of the world.

It is obvious, then, that an interpreter of Shelley is a needed and useful person if he does not try to do too much. On the whole, Mr. Jack and his essay deserve this praise. He is by no means, indeed, an infallible critic ; but he does some useful work of interpretation, and those who find

Shelley's poetry very difficult to follow, will find it rather
less so after reading what Mr. Jack has to say.   Some of the
central facts about Shelley, without which there is no beginning to understand him, he brings out admirably.   Nothing
can be better, for instance, than his last word : ' The secret
of things is what has charm for Shelley, not the things
themselves.'   And this more than anything else is the key,
as he more than once points out, to Shelley's shortcomings
as a poet.   The fatal defect, for instance, of his *Prometheus*
is that the myth in his hands loses its poetic reality, because
he sees too clearly the truth behind the myth.   And the
chief drawback to his great lyrics of love, which are so much
greater than Mr. Jack seems to know, is certainly, as he
says, their tendency to address themselves to an ideal quality,
and not to a beloved person.   All this has been pointed out
before, but never more clearly or more forcibly than here.
And it is the first thing to be grasped by the reader of
Shelley.   Moreover, if it is as essential a part of the poet's
nature as we believe it to have been, it must affect our
estimate, not only of the Shelley who was, but also of the
Shelley who might have been.   Some critics, and Mr. Jack
gives a hint that he agrees with them, have fancied that
one part of the immeasurable loss that befell the world in
the early death of Shelley was the extinction of an unborn
master of the drama.   But could Shelley have ever cast off
that passionate truth-seeking and truth-preaching youth of
his ?   Could he have been content to stand aside, as Shakespeare stands aside, and give us other men's conflicting views
of religion, and politics, and love, and life, without giving
us his own—aye, and passionately pleading for them as the
only truth and salvation ?   No one less tainted by world,
flesh, or devil than Shelley ever took up a pen.   But into
a drama the world and the flesh, at least, if not the devil,
must come ; and they will not come without coaxing.   Had
they enough acquaintance with Shelley at any time to get

as far as knowing his voice? The truth, surely, is that, while a saint may give us a Cenci, with whom we recognize no kinship, no saint could create an Iago, and no vegetarian a Falstaff.

Another general fact about Shelley which, if we would avoid a puzzled disappointment, it is well to get clear before beginning him is his attitude towards Nature. Here, again, Mr. Jack has some good things to say. He is well aware, for instance, that the fact, which has often been pointed out, of the remarkable scientific accuracy of Shelley's descriptions of clouds and winds, lights and shadows, is far from making them better poetry than the less exact work of other poets. He even declares that Shelley's nature poetry, in spite of its truthfulness, is 'markedly inferior' to Wordsworth's. He does not, indeed, put his point quite as clearly as he might, but what he means is that Shelley tries too much to give us the actual naked fact, and with that alone the poet cannot work ; for its statement is science, not poetry, which only arises from the blending of facts with emotion, imagination, temperament, what you will, provided it be something that sets the fact in a new light which is not its own, but comes from outside. But it is hardly here that the difficulty of Shelley's treatment of nature lies. We all have a passion for information, particularly just now, and few people will like Shelley's *Cloud* the less because there is a great deal of scientific fact in it. The difficulty lies in the poem being about a cloud at all. Once more the gulf between us and Shelley lies in the fact that we are of the earth earthy and he is airy of the air. His landscape is not our well-loved trees and flowers, not so much even our worshipped sea and mountains ; it is night and day, dark and dawn, winds and clouds and the movements of elemental air, the stars in their courses, the sun and the moon, not as givers of earthly light, but as circling worlds, immeasurably distant, solitary, and aloof. How much harder to follow a poet into such a region as this than into Wordsworth's hills and lakes and streams, his daffodils and daisies! And note a further result of Shelley's choice of world. Not only is it one that few of us feel really at home in, but it is one of incessant motion. Nothing is still in it, nothing even appears still. Is not part of the vagueness which every one feels in Shelley due to this? Wordsworth's 'everlasting hills' stand and wait in their places till their shapes are fixed in our memories. The poet has time to paint them, and we to know and love his picture. But the winds are invisible and the clouds are unresting, and the attempt to seize such elusive presences results in a poetry that cannot speak much more clearly than music. Music is the proper art of motion, as painting and sculpture of rest; poetry lies between the two, and there are moments when Shelley shows us that it will evaporate into vagueness if forced to live in a world of pure motion, as Leconte de Lisle sometimes showed that when confined to a world of rest it is apt to sink into a lifeless sleep.

For these reasons, and others, Shelley cannot be counted as great a poet of Nature as Wordsworth. He is the greatest of all those who have tried to make themselves the poetic voice of the physical universe; and he has moments of sublime ecstasy which thrill us to the soul. But, good as ecstasy is, we cannot live by it; rather we have to live by something soberer, something more like the Wordsworthian 'admiration, hope, and love'. Besides, we live on the solid earth, not in the wide spaces of the universe. And there is still another drawback to Shelley's subject and method. Poetry deals with action, with events. But the universe is not for us a place of action; much may be done and suffered there, indeed, but not much that we can know anything about. And, therefore, the field it offers to a poet is narrow and soon exhausted, as well as remote and difficult. The strength and greatness, then, of Shelley, do not lie, as Wordsworth's partly lie, in the discovery of a new relation between Nature and Man. He has, indeed, his part in this Wordsworthian task; for wherever he goes he carries spirit with him, and it is only when man sees spirit behind the passing shapes of nature that he can feel his kinship with them. But the essence of Shelley lies in no creed; it lies in the attraction of the most spiritual personality that has ever given itself to the writing of poetry.

Carducci thought Shelley the only modern poet worthy to be carried—and it is Sophocles who carries him—to the Blessed Island which is the abode of the great poets of the past. No one could be a better judge of such a question than the author of *Presso l' urna di Percy Bysshe Shelley*, who was, perhaps, at his death the greatest poet in Europe, and was besides a master of learning and criticism. But poetry is not written exclusively for poets, and it is fair to remember that, unlike as Carducci was to Shelley, they were still both poets. And that means that the peculiar drawbacks of Shelley would be far less felt by Carducci than by the common lover of poetry. Imagination is, of course, stronger in poets than in their readers, and there never was a poet who keeps his readers' imaginations at such high pressure as Shelley. Till one becomes familiar with him, he is the most exhausting of great poets. Only now and then—in *The Cenci*, for instance, in the *Epistle to Maria Gisborne*, and a few other poems—does he deign to keep so much as one foot upon solid earth. He lives among elements and ideas, not among human beings. His mind is not only the most ethereal of minds, far more ethereal than that of his beloved Plato, but it is also the most restless and incoherent, the most impatient of the necessary compromises both of life and of art. No one ever so little understood the truth of Goethe's great saying that the ' direct striving after the Unconditional in this thoroughly conditioned world is a sad mistake '. He himself spoke of his lack of that ' tranquillity which is the attribute and accompaniment of power '. He never exercised

any self-control over his mind, and he had not, like other
poets, a body of readers to control it for him indirectly. He
was always, as Mr. Brock says, ' at the mercy of his subject ';
he would not revise or compress his uninspired passages ; he
has such an overwhelming and hurrying abundance of ideas
and images that they simply fade into each other, leaving
the mind of the reader in an intellectual mist. In this way
he produced an immense quantity of poetry in a very short
time, but, as Mr. Brock says, he 'might have produced half
as much and yet have worked harder. For the test is not
how much verse a poet produces, but how much of it posterity
will read.' But Shelley could not, or would not, take the
advice Keats gave him to practise 'self-concentration', 'serve
Mammon ', and 'be more of an artist'. If he had been able,
the poet of *Adonais* and the *West Wind*, the lyrist who has
no superior and perhaps no equal in any language, would
have not so often lost himself and us in a wilderness of
incoherent verbiage.

All this is true and necessary to be said, and much of it,
with much else, is said by Mr. Brock with admirable insight
and courage. But he and every one who has felt the unique
wonder of Shelley must be conscious of a kind of profanation
in saying such things. Perhaps they are in essence, like the
discussions of the weak points in the poet's character, only
an attempt to explain why Shelley, being so much, was not
also something more. And, in any case, it is what he was
that is the essential truth of all. And as to that there cannot
be much doubt. Never, perhaps, have the highest human
emotions, the exultations, and the agonies of the human
spirit, found such utterance as they found through Shelley.
All their tumult is still in them as they pass into his verse,
and yet the noise and fury of their storm have to our
delighted wonder become a divine harmony of music. Never
was lyric flight so swift as Shelley's, so heavenly high, so
daring, so triumphant. Never—it is the poet's strength as

well as his weakness—are we borne so utterly beyond and above the 'low-thoughted cares' of this earth as in the supernal ecstasies of *Adonais* and of the lyrics of the *Prometheus*. There is no English music like his except that played on Milton's organ; and there it is not that the music is richer so much as that the instrument is one of greater power and compass. In that escape of the spirit which is the special prerogative of music Shelley stands alone. No poet in all the world is so entirely unintelligible to those whose life is a thing of the body only. If the only civilization which rational men can care about is the ascent from the merely bodily life to a life in which the reason and the soul play an ever-increasing part, no poet is more dependent on it than Shelley. There are other poets in whom the ape and the tiger can find their food, but they starve at once on Shelley. Shelley was no more a Christian than he was an ancient Greek; but if we could imagine such a catastrophe as the undoing of all that Greece and Christianity have successively done for the human race, no poet would suffer so instantaneous an eclipse as he. The Barbarians often have a taste for Byron, and sometimes for Pope; the Philistines are apt to lay ugly hands on Milton and Wordsworth and Tennyson; the populace, when it can understand his language, has an affinity with the best of Burns; but neither Barbarians, nor Philistines, nor populace, so long as they remain what they are, will ever touch Shelley. No one ever loved the human race so passionately as he, but he cannot appeal to more than a small fraction of it. For the rest he speaks an unknown tongue. He could not see the future in the present, the spirit in the body, the prophecy of humanity in actual men and women, as Wordsworth saw it, and he suffers as those who deny the incarnation of wisdom have always suffered. No one has so little as he of that sovereign, all-embracing humanity of Shakespeare which, loving and indulging the body as well as the mind and the soul, can force its way into the most unlikely places where no other poetry finds entrance. From all that Shelley stands apart, a pure, untainted spirit in a gross and tainted world, a vision of beauty to those who can see spirits, an ever-working force of hope and love and justice to those minorities to whom in the future, as in the past, the progress of the world will be due. His life seemed to himself a sad one. But it was happier than he knew. For its inspiration was no private joy or fame, but precisely this hope that through his poetry he might become an energy of life to the best elements in human existence. And before the Mediterranean waters closed over his head that hope had become an undying reality.

ANCIENT TRAGEDY AND MODERN IMITATIONS [1]

Has the novel killed its elder sister, the drama ? It sometimes seems so. At any rate, that kind of play which was
for so long as a matter of course one of the literary events
of its year appears to be in the main a thing of the past.
There has never been a half-century since the revival of
letters in which the great poets have had so little to do
with the European theatres as they have had in the last.
The poetic play lingers here and there ; but even in France,
with the exception of Hugo, the greatest poetic names have
not shone on the stage ; in England no man of letters of the
first rank has written much or successfully for the theatre ;
and such names as those of D'Annunzio and Hauptmann
scarcely make Italy and Germany exceptions to the apparent
general rule that the drama is no longer, what it once was,
the most popular and universal medium of expression for
the world's greatest men of letters. There are always individuals who defy all rules ; and in this case there is Ibsen ;
but, as a whole, it may be safely said that our age puts its
best thought and feeling sometimes into lyric poetry, sometimes into prose novels, rarely or never into the drama.
The poet and the theatrical manager have gone different
ways on which they can rarely meet ; and the rival feared
by tutors and governesses as seducing their charges away
from more serious studies is no longer the once dreaded
'stage-play', but the insinuating, all-pervading novel.

[1] *Matthew Arnold's Merope.* To which is appended the *Electra of
Sophocles,* translated by Robert Whitelaw. Edited by J. Churton Collins.
Clarendon Press.

And yet the drama is one of the greatest literary forms, a thing not merely of splendid memories, but of indestructible fascination and interest. The characteristic of the art of the last two or three generations has been its tendency to take the whole sphere of human experience as its province, to call nothing common or unclean, to disdain nothing, to reject nothing, to say anything and everything that exists to be said on any and every subject under the sun. It sometimes seems that the doctrine of selection, once so potent in literature and art, has entirely disappeared. For good and for evil we have been taught the opposite doctrine of a kind of democratic universalism ; any words, any method, any material, any subject, may be properly used in the production of a work of art. Whatever be the amount of truth in this creed, it undoubtedly has its dangers ; and it is one of the advantages of definite forms in literature, like the drama and the sonnet, that they are a certain safeguard against some of these dangers. There is nothing to limit the intolerable verbosity of novelists ; but, when a man sits down to write a sonnet, he knows that if he has anything to say, he must say it at once ; for the fatal fourteenth line will be upon him in a moment, and his opportunity gone. It is the same thing with the drama. Not only is there the limitation that all its words must be spoken words, but there is the invaluable restraint that all must be said and done within a period of two or three hours. The obvious result is that the dramatist cannot afford to waste his strength. Nothing superfluous can be admitted ; all must be concentrated into a single action of dramatic effect. How in these conditions to attain that unity in variety which is called art is the problem of the dramatist. Few literary problems have a longer history or a more perennial interest, and the most recent proof of the permanence of that interest is the volume before us.

It is an experiment, as indeed the preface admits, that

Professor Churton Collins is making in reissuing in one volume the *Merope* of Matthew Arnold and Mr. Whitelaw's translation of the *Electra* of Sophocles. His object is to try to 'bring home to modern readers who are not Greek scholars Attic tragedy in its most perfect form, and in all its characteristics of theme, structure, sentiment, and style'. He has a high opinion of the value of translations even of poetry, and has the courage to say 'with confidence' that 'whoever will read *Merope*, and side by side with it the version of the *Electra* here printed, will, so far as Sophocles is concerned, have come as near to him as nine-tenths of those who study him in the original'. The book is, in fact, another of the many attempts that Professor Collins has made in different ways to give the mass of people who read, especially those who are in some sort students without being in any way scholars, an interest in the finest and greatest literature. Believing that the Greek tragedies are 'the only dramatic masterpieces comparable to Shakespeare's', he is anxious to do what he can to enable the plain reader of Shakespeare to make the comparison. He therefore takes the most formally exact copy of a Greek play ever made by a modern poet, places by its side a version of the Greek tragedy to which it owes most, and prefaces the two by an interesting and instructive critical introduction. This is disfigured by some odd mistakes of writing or printing—such as 'Erectheus', the statement that *Samson Agonistes* is 'one of the sublimiest compositions in the world', a passage on page 6 which is rendered entirely unintelligible by some misprint, and the statement, somewhat startling in English letters without a hint of explanation, that dialogue found its way into Greek tragedy 'by the introduction of the Hypocrites'. But these are details and accidents, however unfortunate. The substance of the preface is a useful account, chiefly after Aristotle, of what the Greek drama was, some allusion to modern imitations

of it and to the points in which they fall short of the play
in which Matthew Arnold ' has had the courage to reproduce
without the smallest modification the exact counterpart of
Attic tragedy in its most perfect shape', and finally an
account of the *Merope* legend and of the various plays that
have dealt with it.

The question is whether all this will really produce the
results so hopefully anticipated by Professor Collins.   Is he
really right in thinking that, for those who cannot approach
the Greek poets by the steep but straight road of the original
language, the best path to recommend is that of the literal
translation or the formally exact copy?   Few scholars, we
fancy, would agree with him in thinking that in *Merope*
Arnold ' has produced a poem which is not only the nearest
approach possible in any modern language to Sophoclean
tragedy, but he has illustrated, as effectively as Sophocles
himself could have done had he written in English, all that
can be achieved in impression by dramatic art working
under the conditions imposed on it by the Greeks'.   And
the disagreement would come from something deeper than
mere impatience at the slovenliness of such a sentence.
For the assertion it makes is really that, if Sophocles had
been an Englishman, he could not have produced anything
more dramatically effective than *Merope*, so long as he kept
to the limitations of the Greek drama.   Does anybody
seriously believe that?   Perhaps Professor Collins might
find a supporter in a certain well-known journalist who
informed his public the other day that nothing will so
much surprise people a hundred years hence as the value
we now attach to the Greek and Roman classics.   Probably
this gentleman has a closer acquaintance with the opinions
of the twenty-first century than he has with the works of
the Greek and Latin poets.   At any rate, Professor Collins,
who is a scholar, will hardly care for such an ally.   But
he must not expect many others.   And, as to the way of

translation being the right road to the ancients, it is curious
that he should have overlooked an interesting expression of
opinion on this subject delivered by the author of *Merope*
himself thirty years after that drama was first published.
In the admirable address on Milton which he gave in
St. Margaret's, Westminster, in 1888, Matthew Arnold takes
occasion to set deliberately aside the very case to which
Professor Collins, like so many before him, appeals as
proving the value of translations. 'The Hebrew compositions,' he says, 'were not in verse, and can be not in-
adequately represented by the grand, measured prose of
our English Bible.' And he continues:—

The verse of the poets of Greece and Rome no translation
can adequately reproduce. Prose cannot have the power of
verse; verse-translation may give whatever of charm is in
the soul and talent of the translator himself, but never the
specific charm of the verse and poet translated. In our race
are thousands of readers, presently there will be millions,
who know not a word of Greek and Latin, and will never
learn these languages. If this host of readers are ever to
gain any sense of the power and charm of the great poets
of antiquity, their way to gain it is not through translations
of the ancients, but through the original poetry of Milton,
who has the like power and charm, because he has the like
great style.

That is, surely, the truth. The ideal, the perfect translation is possible now and then in prose. A Jowett, master
of English, master of Greek, and lifelong disciple of Plato,
can give us a translation in which Plato speaks English.
But that is rare enough in the case of prose, and in the
case of verse it simply does not happen. We at this
moment are tempted to think it has happened in the case
of Mr. Gilbert Murray's wonderful renderings of Euripides.
And perhaps it may have. The progress of the world consists
in each generation's finding a man to do something which
could never be done before. But Mr. Murray must wait to
stand the test of time. Till then there must be an un-

certainty whether the very fact that he seems to us so
perfect is not simply the proof that he has given us, not
Euripides, but ourselves.   In the case, at any rate, of the
great verse translations, which have, to a greater or less
extent, survived that supreme test, FitzGerald's *Omar*, for
instance, or Pope's *Iliad*, it seems plain that they owe their
greatness not to their likeness to the originals, but to their
unlikeness; not to any faithful imitation of the Greek or
the Persian poet, but to the English poet's power of style,
thought, and expression.   The finest of the old strict translations, Cary's *Dante*, for instance, give you not the poet
himself, not Dante, but a very different thing, however
interesting, what Dante thought, said, described, in the
Divina Commedia.   Any reader with a real turn for literature will get a better notion of the 'power and charm' of
Dante the poet from learning by heart the opening of the
third book of *Paradise Lost* than from going through the
whole of Cary's version, admirable and excellent though it
is.   Still, highly as Mr. Collins thinks of the possibilities of
verse translation, that is, perhaps, not his main point.   The
chief reason why he desires to recall attention to Arnold's
Merope and Mr. Whitelaw's *Electra* is to impress on his
readers the formal conditions of the Greek drama.   The
importance of *Merope*, from his point of view, is that
'Arnold has in this drama observed to the letter every
canon laid down by Aristotle, and reflected faithfully
every feature of Attic tragedy'.   But perhaps, even so, the
issue remains much the same.   Any scholar can write a play
limited to two or three actors and a chorus, and keeping to
all the rules explained by Aristotle; but the question is
whether the thing when he has accomplished it is alive
any more than literal translations commonly are.   These
formal conditions are the easiest thing in the world to
reproduce; but, after all, an English Alcaic ode on a
Horatian subject is not Horace, nor is the most correct

arrangement of 'parodos', 'epeisodion', 'stasimon', and 'exodos' at all the same thing as a Sophoclean tragedy. When the souls of dead poets return to life it is not by their old clothes, or even by their former bodily shape, that we are to recognize them, but by the undying spirit which creates, accepts, and uses all forms in succession.

Most people, then—we think, even most admirers of Arnold—will feel that *Merope* is not the most satisfactory proof he gave of his faith in the Greeks. Facts are useful things, and *Merope*, like a plastic cast, states all the facts about its original; shape and attitude and measurements, they are all there. But art and poetry demand more than facts; they demand life; and life is the one thing which no *Merope* or plastic cast can give. For that the wise plan is again to turn to Milton, in spite of some slight discouragement on the part of Professor Collins. Goethe said that *Samson Agonistes* had 'more of the antique spirit than any production of any other modern poet'. No doubt there is, as Professor Collins says, a very strong Hebraic tinge in it, but its choruses are, after all, hardly graver in their outlook upon life than those of the *Oedipus*, the *Antigone*, or the *Agamemnon*. Nor is it really true, as he thinks, that 'the power and impressiveness of Milton's last work is not what it possesses in common with its formal models, but what distinguishes it from them'. On the contrary, it owes its strange impressiveness very largely to being all through, as it were, a devotional act, an act of religion, to its choral character, with a suggestion of a grave processional music accompanying it, to its strictly confined unity of action, to its high disdain of all trivial or comic relief; and these are all features which it has in common with the Greeks and in contrast with Shakespeare. To read it and to get from it one's conception of Greek tragedy is, no doubt, to give to Greek tragedy a more sombre colouring as well as a greater religious depth than it actually possessed;

but no more formally exact copy, such as *Merope*, can rival
Samson for a moment in fixing upon the modern reader the
three central qualities of Greek drama—unity of plot, music,
and religion.

Still, though *Merope* is not the best key to Sophocles,
though it is often hampered rather than helped by its
almost slavish adherence to Greek precedents, though it is
more an exercise than an original work, yet it is fair to
remember that it is the exercise of one who was a poet as
well as a scholar. He has, indeed, followed his originals in
some features which we could well spare. In his original
preface to the play he declares that the business of the
Chorus, as the Greeks employed it, was to play the part of
'the ideal spectator'; 'to combine, to harmonize, to deepen'
for the ordinary spectator 'the feelings naturally excited in
him by the sight of what was passing on the stage'. Probably this is a fair account of what was aimed at. But every
one remembers cases in which the comments of the Chorus
are strangely lacking in such quickness of sympathy as one
would suppose even the dullest and least interested spectator
could not escape feeling. This is commonest in the dialogues ;
but it occurs sometimes in the songs, as for instance in the
Oedipus, where the paean of joy and hope sung by the Chorus
on the very eve of the discovery, when Jocasta has already
guessed the worst and the Chorus itself has expressed its fore-
bodings, is to our ears something between an outrage and an
impossibility. Who could care at such a moment whether
Oedipus would prove a native of Thebes or not? In the
exactness of his imitation Arnold has given his Chorus a
touch of the same insensibility. The death of Aepytus, the
only son of their beloved mistress, leaves the Messenian
maidens free to chant the praises of the peace which may
result from the destruction of Merope's hopes and the ruin
of their party ! It would surely be as dramatic, if we
suppose Charles Edward to have been suddenly drowned

in 1745, to bring on the stage a company of Jacobite ladies rejoicing in the quiet the country would derive from the final establishment of the Hanoverian dynasty. Part of what strikes us as so incongruous may no doubt be due to the difference between Greek and Christian feeling; but part must surely also be due to the traditions which hampered the Greek dramatists in dealing with the Chorus, and made it so difficult for them to give it a really human share in the action, or in the sympathies it should naturally arouse. And this part might fairly have been ignored by a modern imitator, as might another characteristic of the ancient chorus retained by Arnold, its obscurity, and its extravagant demand on the spectator's acquaintance with legendary lore.

But, in spite of all drawbacks, *Merope* is the work of a poet. And a real poet may do what he pleases; whatever he does he cannot conceal the poetry that is in him. Even if *Merope* be too mechanical a copy of the Greeks, even if it fall far short of the high energy of Milton's *Samson*, still it is not for nothing that a man like Arnold had steeped himself in the Greek spirit. The English reader may see in *Merope* reflections of many of the great qualities of Greek drama; its gravity, for instance, its severity, its scornful neglect of small realisms and prettinesses, its tenseness, its unity. But, just as *Samson* itself, whatever it owes to the Greeks, owes more to the lofty genius of Milton, so *Merope* owes its best, not to the poet who inspired it, but to him who wrote it. It is true he could not find in such formal bonds the free play for his powers that he found in telling, in his own way, the tale of Sohrab or of Tristram. But he has thrown all his sympathetic tenderness into the character of Merope herself; and he has found expression for a great deal of his most personal reflections on human life and destiny in the utterances he has placed in the mouth of the Chorus. What could be at once more Sophoclean,

and at the same time more peculiarly characteristic of
Arnold, than the choral song which precedes the first
appearance of Aepytus? Its verse is, as so often with
Arnold, rather stumbling and heavy-gaited; and the thinking quality in it too far overbalances the musical; but how
quiet, wise, and grave it is! How like Arnold! And if it
had but more music and more story, how like the Greeks!

Much is there which the sea
Conceals from man, who cannot plumb its depths.
Air to his unwing'd form denies a way,
And keeps its liquid solitudes unscaled.
Even earth, whereon he treads,
So feeble is his march, so slow,
Holds countless tracts untrod.

But more than all unplumb'd,
Unscaled, untrodden, is the heart of man.
More than all secrets hid, the way it keeps.
Nor any of our organs so obtuse,
Inaccurate, and frail,
As those wherewith we try to test
Feelings and motives there.

Yea, and not only have we not explored
That wide and various world, the heart of others,
But even our own heart, that narrow world
Bounded in our own breast, we hardly know,
Of our own actions dimly trace the causes.
Whether a natural obscureness, hiding
That region in perpetual cloud,
Or our own want of effort, be the bar.

Therefore—while acts are from their motives judged,
And to one act many most unlike motives,
This pure, that guilty, may have each impelled—
Power fails us to try clearly if that cause
Assign'd us by the actor be the true one;
Power fails the man himself to fix distinctly
The cause which drew him to his deed,
And stamp himself, thereafter, bad or good.

Or, to give a less prosaic specimen, more Greek, less purely
Arnold:—

Knowing he did it, unknowing pays for it.
Unknowing, unknowing,
Thinking atoned-for
Deeds unatonable,
Thinking appeased
Gods unappeasable,
Lo, the ill-fated one,
Standing for harbour,
Right at the harbour-mouth
Strikes with all sail set
Full on the sharp-pointed
Needle of ruin!

But, to return to our text, it is still not to *Merope*, even at
its best, that we must go if we would come close to that
authentic fire of Greek tragedy which glows but rarely
sparkles.   For that we must go elsewhere; and, in English,
to the author of—

All is best, though we oft doubt,
What the unsearchable dispose
Of Highest Wisdom brings about,
And ever best found in the close.
Oft he seems to hide his face,
But unexpectedly returns,
And to his faithful champion hath in place
Bore witness gloriously; whence Gaza mourns,
And all that band them to resist
His uncontrollable intent.
His servants he, with new acquist
Of true experience from this great event,
With peace and consolation hath dismissed,
And calm of mind, all passion spent.

SWINBURNE'S SCOTCH TRILOGY [1]

THE historical play is the young poet's besetting sin. It seems so easy and it is so hard. It seems such an advantage to have a great and moving subject ready made, and it almost always turns out that what is made by history is no longer makeable by art. Art needs before all things a material that can be shaped. The marble that was too hard for the chisel could not serve the sculptor. The dramatist is an artist too, and needs a material on which his formative energy can be employed. But history, so far as we accurately know it, is a thing which has received its final form. Even the gods cannot undo or remake the past. What a task then for the poet when he takes for his subject a tale like the tale of Mary Stuart!

The truth seems to be that, while legend is a help to the playwright, history is most often a hindrance. Legend gives him all the help of august names which wake great memories at once, quicken the reader's expectation, attune his ears for the reception of high music, and stimulate his imagination. And it still leaves the poet a free man. Within certain limits, and no true artist wishes for the unlimited, the Greek dramatists could remould as they pleased the great tales of Oedipus or Agamemnon or Heracles. Their greatest triumphs lay in that field. No one will rank the *Persae* with the *Prometheus*, even though the Persian side of that piece of history left Aeschylus almost the freedom of the unknown. And, even for the

[1] *The Tragedies of Algernon Charles Swinburne.* In five volumes. Volumes II, III, and IV. *Chastelard, Bothwell, Mary Stuart.* Chatto and Windus.

one supreme master of history or drama, above all law as
he may seem to be, the same law still really holds. Even his
Titan strength cannot bend the ascertained facts of the
reign of a Richard or a Henry as he can the shadowy story
of a Lear, a Macbeth, or a Hamlet. It is notable that he
hardly ever went to an absolutely untried field. Probably
he never thought about the theory of the thing; but his
instinctive genius told him that art of all kinds demands
a combination of the familiar and the strange. In music,
in painting, in poetry, wherever we look, it is the same.
The human mind asks at once for variety and for rest, for
the new and for the old. What is exactly like a thing
we have seen before does not interest us; what is entirely
unlike everything we have seen before disgusts and repels
us. So Shakespeare felt that the ideal subject for drama
was one of which his public would know just something
but not too much, something by which he would be sure
beforehand of their interest while he would himself retain
a free hand in telling his tale. In the Histories even he
could not shake himself quite free; and the dull debates
reprinted from the Chroniclers, which disfigure many of
them, are the result.

Mr. Swinburne is not Shakespeare, and still less than
Shakespeare is he any exception to these general laws.
It is interesting to read these old plays, because it is interesting to read everything that comes from the pen of a
man of genius. Mary of Scotland, though she has somehow
brought no more luck to her poets than she won for herself,
is still a subject about which it is not easy to be uninteresting. And there are pages here and there in these
long plays, where that wonderful woman, the secret of
whose charm is really as much lost to us as the beauty of
her face, does emerge for a moment to dazzle, to fascinate,
to fill us with a horror of surprise, the terror of a thing not
in truth altogether human as we understand humanity.

But they are small lights lost in large and very dark places, gems buried among wildernesses of verbiage in which uninteresting minor characters make speeches a page long, John Knox, indeed, who makes very few appearances in the plays, turning one of them to such powerful use as to continue a single unbroken discourse for ten pages! But, even if all these wearinesses were got rid of, the fact remains that the interest of the plays lies neither in Mary, nor in Bothwell, nor in Darnley, nor in Mary Beaton, nor even in Chastelard, but in Mr. Swinburne. He is a great lyric and elegiac poet, a fountain of fiery verse, and he has stamped for ever with his imperishable genius some of the universal themes of human feeling, love and death, childhood and liberty, sunrise and the sea. The essence of the man is not dramatic at all; his gift is essentially the pouring out in immortal music of his personal faith and feelings about man, and human life, and the visible earth. It is an accident of little importance that on a few great occasions he found it easiest to cast all this into dramatic shape. It is still essentially a lyrical memory that we all have of Atalanta, and indeed of all his plays. What we carry away from them is not so much any contest of differing persons, any great dramatic situation, as an unforgettable strain of love and fate and death, man's beauty and the beauty of the earth and the swift descent of the doom that divides them. Everywhere it is the same; whatever form his work takes the lyric note is dominant. In pure music he never rose higher than in the great *Atalanta* chorus; he has no finer outburst of the lyric soul within him than the splendid praise of love with which the narrative tragedy of *Tristram* opens. There is no such poetry in these Scotch plays; but the best things in them are still things in which we hear the poet's own voice, not things in which we forget him in his characters. It is interesting to see how characteristically itself that voice was from the very first.

Chastelard appeared in 1865, but the boy who published it
was already the unique personality who was to have the
glory of being the greatest living English poet. The note
is a little thin and young; but it is unmistakable, his own
and no one's else :—

> I wonder men die south; meseems all France
> Smells sweet with living, and bright breath of days
> That keep men far from dying ;—

or the song that follows :—

> Between the sunset and the sea
> My love laid hands and lips on me ;
> Of sweet came sour, of day came night,
> Of long desire came brief delight :
> Ah love, and what thing came of thee
> Between the sea-downs and the sea ?

No one who knows the later volumes could mistake the
author of that. And who but Mr. Swinburne would have
put just these words into Mary's mouth as she questions
herself about Elizabeth ?

> By my faith,
> Fain would I know, what knowing not of her now
> I muse upon and marvel, if she have
> Desire or pulse or passion of true heart
> Fed full from natural veins, or be indeed
> All bare and barren all as dead men's bones
> Of all sweet nature and sharp seed of love,
> And those salt springs of life, through fire and tears
> That bring forth pain and pleasure in their kind
> To make good days and evil, all in her
> Lie sere and sapless as the dust of death.

It is these things, the poet's and not the dramatist's, that
make the pleasure of these plays—the peculiar rhythm of
the blank verse, with its special affection for a pause on an
unaccented seventh syllable, the use of alliteration, the con-
trasted pairs of opposites always found together ('sweet
nature and sharp seed', 'fire and tears', 'pain and pleasure',
good days and evil'), the effect as of something utterly

simple, final, and almost elemental produced by the bare
austerity of whole lines of monosyllables, such as have always
marked Mr. Swinburne's finest moments.

So we make moan for the old sweet days—

> Love, that what time his own hands guard his head,
> The whole world's wrath and strength shall not strike
>   dead—

> Live thou and take thy fill of days and die
> When thy day comes; and make not much of death
> Lest ere thy day thou reap an evil thing—

> And now for God's sake kiss me once or twice
> And let me go : for the night gathers me,
> And in the night shall no man gather fruit.

So, in these plays, too, the greatest moment of their greatest
character, the only character into which the poet seems to
enter with his whole heart, produces such lines as :—

> I know not : men must love you in life's spite :
> For you will always kill them : man by man
> Your lips will bite them dead ; yes, though you would,
> You shall not spare one ; all will die of you :
> I cannot tell what love shall do with these,
> But I for all my love shall have no might
> To help you more, mine arms and hands no power
> To fasten on you more. This cleaves my heart,
> That they shall never touch your body more.
> But for your grief—you will not have to grieve ;
> For being in such poor eyes so beautiful
> It must needs be as God is more than I
> So much more love he hath of you than mine :
> Yea, God shall not be bitter with my love,
> Seeing she is so sweet.

Here in this, perhaps the greatest speech in all the
Trilogy, out of 137 words only one is of three syllables, and
only seven are of two syllables, the remaining 129 being all
scanned as monosyllables. Of course, this use of monosyllables for the saying of things that seem almost too
great for speech at all is not peculiar to Mr. Swinburne.

Vex not his ghost: O let him pass: he hates him,
That would upon the rack of this tough world
Stretch him out longer.

But there is no poet of whom it is more characteristic than
it is of the author of *Tristram* and *Atalanta.*

These Scotch plays will certainly not be among the best
remembered creations of their author's. They are altogether without some of the things through which he has
climbed to his highest heights. The sea, which in
Tristram is scarcely forgotten for a moment, is in these
three volumes barely mentioned once or twice. There are
no children in them, except the baby James VI, unhappiest
baby in all history, and to him there are only the most
heartless allusions. And there is only John Knox to give
once or twice some poor suggestion of the splendid out-
bursts of the love of liberty and country and hatred of
tyrants and slaves that were to play such a great part in
later volumes. It all comes back to the same thing. Mr.
Swinburne is a lyric poet and not a dramatist; and the loss
of these three volumes would hurt his ultimate fame far less
than the loss of one such lyric as *The Eve of Revolution*, or
Super Flumina Babylonis, or *The Oblation*, or *Ex Voto*, or
A Child's Laughter, or the three stanzas that came from him
at the death of Victor Hugo. Towards all these things,
liberty, and love, and the sea, and childhood, and death,
Mr. Swinburne's is a passionately personal attitude, and
that is the same thing as saying that it is one whose
natural way of utterance is not the drama but the lyric
ode.

A MODERN PLATONIST [1]

WE live in an age in which, till recently at any rate, the battle has been more than commonly believed to be to the strong. Materialism, *Realpolitik*, business methods, survival of the fittest—these are the things that apparently rose on the ruins of the optimistic idealizing Liberalism of the mid-nineteenth century. Mommsen replaced Niebuhr and Arnold, Mr. Kipling became a kind of national Laureate to a people who possess Wordsworth and Shelley, the young 'intellectuals' who formerly sat at the feet of John Stuart Mill took to sitting at those of Nietzsche. The tendency has been reflected even in style. The pulpit thunders of Ruskin leave no more room for doubt than a Papal decree. Delicacy, fine shades of thought, the hesitations and distinctions that belong to the perception that life is an elusive, many-sided business, requiring very tactful handling, are necessarily excluded from these sweeping pontifical utterances. So with Carlyle who in some ways anticipates Nietzsche, though he lived with Mill. Pity he has, but never tolerance. His method of bringing his opponent to his own position is always to knock him down and drag the dead body to the required spot, never to feel his way tentatively to the place where the opponent stands so as to let him see that there is a path leading from the one to the other, and to tempt him to follow back along it. 'Ye know

<hr />

[1] *The Works of Walter Pater.* New Library Edition. Vol. I, The Renaissance ; Vols. II and III, Marius the Epicurean ; Vol. IV, Imaginary Portraits ; Vol. V, Appreciations. To be completed in ten volumes. Macmillan.

not what spirit ye are of.' The very men who most hated and scorned the age of 'bagmen', and its high priest, Macaulay, were still full of one of its worst characteristics, its positive and blustering self-assurance. Not Macaulay himself is fuller than they of that conviction, which properly belongs only to the uneducated, that things are quite plain, and statements about them are to be made categorically without doubts, cautions, or reservations. The very tongues that most loudly rebuked democracy and materialism did so with the confident violence of a street orator.

These were the voices that all could hear, that could not have been heard by all unless they had had in them something with which all felt some sort of kinship. But meanwhile there was another side of the life of the time, a critical, questioning, balancing side, turning over all these loud assertions and testing them by the dry light of a reason which insists on weighing all things, of a sympathy which is ready to believe that opposite opinions have each some reconciling element of truth in them. Of this other side no man was more representative than Walter Pater. Minds like his can never achieve a popular success. They have neither the merits nor the defects that make for that; neither the revealing lightning-flash of genius nor the darkness which generally precedes and follows it; neither, it would be more exact to say, the piercing vision which not only sees a thing, but makes it alive, gives it motion, force, name, personality, all the gifts that can only be given by creative power; nor, on the other hand, that blindness which is the companion of the vision, the blindness of genius averting the eye from all but that which it is its especial and immediate business to see. They try to look at the world from all possible sides, to prove all things; and, if they end in Montaigne's *Que sçais-je?* it is not necessarily in Montaigne's spirit of amused indifference, as of a person playing a game, whose object is not to win it but to pass the afternoon away pleasantly, but often rather, and certainly in Pater's own case, in the spirit, as he says, of the Platonic Socrates, with whom the right sort of doubt was 'nothing less than a religious duty or service'.

This was just the part that Pater played, in his own field, all his life. That he played it in the end with success, the only kind of success such a man was likely to care about, securing the attention of people who felt that he helped them to understand life and to live, is proved by this new edition of his works. It is not, one may be sure, brought out for the ordinary member of the circulating libraries. Neither the men who want to get through a day at the seaside, nor the ladies who have nothing to do when they have finished feeding the parrot, are likely to read Pater. When he is read at all it is by people who make a practice of considering their ways, and not their own only, but the ways of the human spirit, the way of thought, the way of art, the way of religion. Many such people find that the things Pater had to say on these questions are among the most fruitful, the most suggestive, and even, just because of their cautious economy of assertion, the most convincing that have been said in our own generation or in the last. They therefore read him, and read him again, and that is the same thing as saying that they wish to buy his books and keep them. And hence, no doubt, the new edition of an author who could never be exactly popular.

The old notion that Pater was an epicurean and a hedonist may be supposed now to be finally dismissed, though there were some strange indications of its persistence in Mr. Algernon Cecil's *Six Oxford Thinkers*. The reading of a very few chapters of any of his later works would be sufficient to disprove it; 'χαλεπὰ τὰ καλά' is their note; and their atmosphere much nearer that of the cloister than that of any of the abodes of the Epicureans, whether palace

or pigsty. The truth is that the key to the understanding
of the author of *The Renaissance,* of *Marius,* and of all that
lies between them is always to be looked for in the same
place, in the philosopher who was so much more than a
philosopher, in Plato. Pater is only a fragment of Plato,
of course. No one could be further than he, for instance,
from Plato's incomparable lightness of style. For that
gracious ease, as of a river flowing delightedly in the sunshine, Pater substitutes a style which is often of involved
and halting obscurity, turning and returning upon itself
in endless coils of hesitation. It is true that he writes with
a felicity and precision of phrase which makes it always an
intellectual pleasure to read him, and, more than that, that
his language seems at its best to have a kind of emotional
kinship with its subject; but high merits as these are, they
cannot prevent our seeing that he is altogether without
some of the most necessary virtues of a writer of prose, has
no swiftness, little beauty of motion, far too little clarity
of construction. '*The Apology . . .* we may naturally take
for a sincere version of the actual words of Socrates; closer
to them, we may think, than the Greek record of spoken
words, however important, the speeches in Thucydides, for
instance, by the admission of Thucydides himself, was wont
to be.' How structureless, how top-heavy it is, all that
long sentence crushing the last four unimportant little
words with its weight, while they add nothing to the sense
and scarcely seem to have any business there at all. There
are too many of such sentences in Pater; and they, if there
were no greater things to do it, would show that the servant
is, in a good many ways, not as his master. But still the
essential Pater is the Platonist.

What, after all, is a Platonist? Let Pater himself give
the answer. He remarks that there are two opposite
Platonic traditions in the history of philosophy, the one
resting in an intuitive assurance of the highest acts of

knowledge, enjoying a 'vision' of the truth, the other
balancing and measuring and questioning, but ending in
an 'Academic' suspension of judgement. Aristotle, who
embraces all actions of the mind, is on the whole the father
of the first tradition which develops through the Neo-
Platonists to mediaeval mystics and modern poets in a line
which stretches from Plotinus to Wordsworth. The other
tradition, coming straight from Plato's own Academy, finds
its representatives in such names as those of Lucian and
Montaigne. The first line represents the Parmenidean side
of Plato, the firm faith in an absolute and ultimate truth,
the doctrine of the Ideas; the second, the inconclusive
wanderings of the human mind as it moves this way and
that through the long course of the Platonic Dialogues.
Now, the point is that Pater represents both traditions. He
has the temper of mind characteristic of the Dialogues,
that which has an appearance of never forcing the argument but letting it go its own way, lying in wait for the
truth to descend by some act of grace upon the discussion,
hurrying nothing, anticipating nothing. But he has also,
and more and more as he grew older, the instinctive and
unshakeable assurance of the ultimate truths which under-
lie the argument and make it real. Beauty, truth, goodness—nothing ever shook his faith in the supreme reality
of these. They are his ideas, his patterns laid up in the
heavens, and all the tentative wanderings of his mind, all
its hesitations, only hung on the difficulty of finding them
amid the confusion of their earthly counterparts and
shadows. He spent his life in writing essays, and he says
somewhere that the essay, 'a little trench or hole which
they dig to search for ore,' as an old dictionary defines it,
is the proper literary form of an age like ours, in which
truth is realizable chiefly as 'the elusive effect of a personal experience'. His notion of it is that of a kind of
dialogue with oneself; a formulated and public part of

that 'continuous company we keep with ourselves through life'; and, with such subjects as he chose for his continuous self-questioning, he might well have justified himself for so spending his days and years by those words of Plato's Glaucon:—'Well, for the wise, at any rate, the proper time to give to such discussions is the whole of life.' The whole of life, because the complete solution, the answer that does not itself ask another question, is never reached; but also— and this is the other side of the Platonic tradition—the whole of life, because there is never a doubt that a true and final solution exists. And even for a higher reason still; for the reason that he, too, no doubt felt, as his own Marius felt that summer morning at Tibur, that the long dialogue was not, after all, with himself alone, but shared all the while with another companion, an unfailing invisible companion, at his side all the way through; one that might, for him as for the dying Marius, lay a friendly hand upon his shoulder amid the obscurities of the world, and make some explanation of them at the last.

There is another thing. It was no small part of Plato's philosophic achievement to have fashioned a meeting-place for 'the one' and 'the many', the grey, motionless shadow of the Parmenidean unity and the restless, many-sided, many-coloured flux of Heraclitus. A man of thought and a man of religion, he must needs bring his world together under one central Idea: a lover of art, a liver of life, he cannot be content with an abstraction; his Idea must take visible shape, must play a hundred visible parts in a complex world. This last side of himself, however much he may appear sometimes to pass upon it a philosophic condemnation, was, one cannot but feel, very real in Plato. Certainly it was very real in Pater, nor did he ever desire to deny or conceal it. The note of his first and in some respects his most remarkable book may be given in a single sentence of its preface—'Our education becomes complete

in proportion as our susceptibility to these impressions'
(i. e. the impressions of pleasure to be derived from nature,
art, and human life) 'increases in depth and variety'. And
the business of the essays which it contains is to draw out,
by a kind of Socratic midwifery, the special birth of meaning, the special intellectual pleasure which lies hidden in
each of the subjects with which it deals. But also, like
Plato, and even in this book, the most detached, the most
purely aesthetic of his works, he desires a unity in his
diversity. Part of the attraction which throws him into
the study of that age of the Renaissance is that it is one
of the rare epochs in which the many interests of the intellectual world—'art and poetry, philosophy and the religious
life, and that other life of refined pleasure and action in the
open places of the world,' all 'combine in one complete
type of general culture'. And all through his work there
runs that increasing note of reconciliation. Human life,
he more and more sees, is a whole : all that the human
mind can embrace must somehow and somewhere find its
unity. Plato may banish poets and speak unkindly of art,
but all through the world's history he has been honoured
and loved by poets and artists at least as much as by philo-
sophers and saints. And Pater may begin by an appearance of pure aestheticism, of Hellenic aloofness from moral
preoccupations, but that pressing need of unity will draw
him on till it comes to be his especial business to interpret
art in terms of thought and still more of religion, to clothe
philosophy and religion in a human garb of colour and
feeling and varied life. What is his *Marius* but an attempt
to trace ' the one in the many' of the human spirit, the likeness between the thoughts of a young Roman of the second
century and a young Englishman of the nineteenth, the
links that unite all religions, the natural, almost imper-
ceptible, progress which in those days of Marcus Aurelius
a devout mind might make from Paganism to Christianity?

For Pater's unity is not one of lifeless immobility, but that of a prôcess, or rather of a growing organism; so that in the field of literature he will once, by a curious freak, dare to say that the chief use of studying the old masters is the help they give in interpreting the new. But, whatever we may think of that, his controlling desire of unity is everywhere evident. He is interested in Goethe as illustrating the union of the subjectivity and adventure of the romantic spirit with the rationality of Hellenism; he delights, in his *Greek Studies*, especially *Demeter*, in finding among the Greeks traces of things commonly denied to them, the Christian ' worship of sorrow ' and the romantic power of extracting beauty out of things strange and painful; and all through *Plato and Platonism* he is for ever using Hebrew and Christian language, applying *sitivit anima mea in Deum, in Deum vivum* to Socrates, closing his account of the violently attained unity of the Platonic Republic with ' that they all may be one ', often bringing in such words as ' sacramental ' and ' penitential ', yet not forcing any parallel, but letting the mere fitness of the alien words bear its silent witness to the human kinship of Jew and Greek, to the ordered, harmonious, not unnatural progress of the world.

This is, at any rate, one aspect of Pater, and perhaps not the least interesting. In a time of loud voices and much eloquent striving and crying, art scorning morals and morals denouncing art, the Church anathematizing the criticism of culture, culture dreading the obscurantism of the Church, Pater felt his way along, through hesitations and scruples, to a unity for which no serious effort of the human spirit could be an object either of scorn or of dread or of denunciation. He was the high priest of the artistic world of his day; but he was also a Puritan, an ascetic of the asceticism which, as he liked to relate, was practised in Sparta and took its place in the ideal of the Hellenic world through the immortal pages of Plato.

EDWARD FITZGERALD

It will be a hundred years next Wednesday[1] since Edward FitzGerald was born at Bredfield. When he died, more than twenty-five years ago, no one thought that his would be one of the names most affectionately and admiringly remembered when the centenary of that *annus mirabilis*, 1809, came round. He had no fame in his lifetime, and no expectation or desire of fame after his death. But he had not been long dead when it began to come to him. Tennyson's dedication to *Tiresias*, written before his friend died, and the epilogue added to that poem after the news of his death had come, were perhaps the first things that told the great public that there was such a man as FitzGerald; other voices followed; and the *Letters and Literary Remains*, issued by Dr. Aldis Wright in 1889, had not been long published before it was admitted on all hands that we had lost in Edward FitzGerald one of the finest poets of the nineteenth century, one of the most delightful of English letter-writers, and a man of rare originality of mind and charm of character. His translation of *Omar Khayyam*, hitherto the secret pleasure of the literary elect, became almost a poem of the streets, quoted and parodied, delivered over to the popular reciters and the fashionable illustrators. Its most aggressive devotees formed themselves into a club bearing its name, dined and made speeches, planted Persian roses on their poet's grave, and behaved generally in a fashion scarcely likely, it would seem, to gratify the solitary, humorous, almost disdainful spirit of FitzGerald. America, too, has taken up the torch, took it up, in fact, before England did, and it flames—shall we say flares?—even wilder and

[1] March 31, 1909.

N 2

windier on that side of the Atlantic than it does on this. And meanwhile the sober prose of the catalogue of the British Museum records more than fifty editions of *Omar*, and our posthumous Academy, the English Men of Letters Series, has summoned the poet into the company of the Immortals, with Mr. Arthur Benson to introduce him and pronounce his praise.

Some of this has not been very wisely or appropriately done, nor by very wise or appropriate doers. The scholar and the Bohemian, often so alike superficially, are essentially wide apart as the poles; and it is strange that FitzGerald, a scholar and an intellectual aristocrat, if there ever was one, should have had to bear so much noisy laudation from ecstatic Bohemians. It is the essence of scholarship to walk always in the great tradition; it is the essence of Bohemianism to be for ever making a dust by the attempt to kick tradition out of the way. It is of the essence of aristocracy to practise an economy of the emotions; it is of the essence of Bohemianism to do both its laughing and its crying aloud and in the streets. FitzGerald was eccentric enough in externals, but no one who knew him ever forgot for a moment that he was most emphatically an English gentleman, with all the essential reserve and dignity of the part. The 'hidalgo' in him would have made him turn a very stiff back on the impertinences of gushing criticism or journalistic gossip; and one may be sure that many of the pilgrims who have made their way to the Little Grange in the last twenty years have been very fortunate in not finding its 'laird' at home. What would have happened if they had found him and got into talk with him about books is a pleasant subject of speculation. For, by some curious freak of fate, the loudest of his worshippers have constantly been recruited from what may be called the 'modernists' of the literary world, men, and especially women, who have nothing but impatient scorn for the education of the public schools and Universities, who resent the authoritative yoke of the centuries and the classics, and lavish their loudest superlatives, at worst on some mere novelist of the hour, at best on some contemporary 'spirit of the age' such as Ibsen, or Nietzsche, or D'Annunzio. Nothing in the whole world of intellect and taste could be less like FitzGerald, whose mind took its permanent shape at Cambridge, whose literary friends were all, or almost all, scholars of the University type like Tennyson and Thompson, Cowell and Dr. Wright, whose studies lay almost entirely among the old classics, Greek or Roman, English or Spanish or Persian, who was so ultra-conservative in his likings that he found even Browning and George Eliot too modern for him, who admitted, as he says, no poems into his paradise but 'such as breathe content and virtue'.

These things are fame's surprises which she distributes as she will. But poets must not hope to choose their admirers or even their readers. Goethe, it is said, liked to think he wrote for girls, but he has turned out to be pre-eminently the poet of grown men. Schiller set himself to address men of thought and reading, and his centenary found him the poet of the governess and the schoolroom. The moral is, perhaps, that the less a poet thinks about his future fame the less likely he is to be deceived. And certainly no one ever thought less than FitzGerald. But the fame remains, an outstanding fact, asking explanation. What is it that makes that birth at Bredfield in 1809 a memorable event now that a hundred years have passed over it?

The principal element in the memorability is, of course, the great version of Omar. Without that FitzGerald would have died unknown; with it he was very slow in winning any general recognition. It had been printed a dozen years and more before his friend Carlyle so much as heard of it; and when he did he could still speak of its author with a sort of kindly condescension as a 'peaceable, affectionate,

and ultra-modest man' of an 'innocent *far-niente* life', and
note a letter of his as a connecting link between 'Omar, the
Mahometan Blackguard, and Oliver Cromwell, the English
Puritan'. So little did he understand that he was writing
of a poem that in thirty years would have more readers
than any book of his own! Tennyson, who knew a poem
when he saw one, could, indeed, not fail to declare that he
knew 'no version done In English more divinely well'.
But even he scarcely seems to have suspected how much
more than a 'version' the poem was, or perceived that Fitz-
Gerald had projected into the old Persian poet much that
had never been his—projected himself, in fact, and more
than himself, a great part of the mind of that generation of
which he proved so intimate an interpreter for all his air
of standing aside from its doings altogether. It never
struck Tennyson that the wistful agnosticism of Omar,
always seeking an answer to the great riddle but never
finding it, forced to acquiesce in its own ignorance, was as
exactly the voice of a very large part of England in the
eighties and nineties as his own *In Memoriam*, an agnosticism
that would not rest in negation but fought its way to an
answer of faith, was of an equally large part of England in
the fifties and sixties. But that was, of course, the real
secret of the popular success the poem ultimately attained.
People who knew nothing of literature, and could have no
opinion as to whether verses were or were not made
'divinely well', found in Omar their own doubts and fears
and difficulties. The books that are widely read outside
the narrow literary world are always those in which people
find themselves. It is a commonplace that the author who
wins immediate success is the man who says to perfection
what everybody around is wishing to say but cannot. Such
authors are not always the greatest. Milton and Wordsworth were not among them. They had in consequence to
wait. But when a man of real power catches the very

breath and spirit of his age, as Pope caught it in his pseudo-moral, popular-philosophic poems, as Scott caught it in the wisely-tempered romanticism of his novels, the success is instantaneous and overwhelming. FitzGerald's success was obviously less immediate and less universal. His *Omar* was first printed in 1859, and it was almost thirty years later that it began to be a popular poem. But when its day came it so exactly fitted the needs of that generation that it lay for a time on every table and its stanzas were in every mouth.

One curious result of its popularity has been to cause a grave injustice to the poet. The epicurean and sensualist side of Omar, tempered as it is in the poem by what is far above sensualism, the serious preoccupation with the greatest of all questions, has yet fixed itself somehow in the minds of people and attached itself most unfairly to FitzGerald. People of the aesthetic-hedonist persuasion have claimed him as a kind of patron saint. His name ought to be cleared of all that. No one was ever less of the luxurious hedonist than Edward FitzGerald. All his life he lived simply, almost barely, not laborious days certainly, but at any rate days that utterly scorned the delights that are dear to the hedonist. He was so unworldly about money that he could take no further interest in his marrying friends when he found they were to be so rich as to have £500 a year! He made his home deliberately in such very unhedonistic spots as Boulge and Woodbridge. If anybody is inclined to confuse the life of leisure with that of luxury, let him read FitzGerald's letters. Let him see a way of living that reduces necessities to the minimum and gives the time and money gained by their suppression to friend-ship and affection, to nature and books, to quiet and solitude and meditation. It is not a life every one could live, but the reason of that is much more often that people are below it than that they are above it. He called it himself a life of 'visionary inactivity', and the visionary quality in it, the quality that made the power of the poet or the charm and distinction of the man, was only made possible by the inactivity. He took no pride in the one or the other, and paid all honour to the 'useful and virtuous activity' of others; but he came to see that his part was not that, but to stand and wait and judge. In his early years he might be vexed at seeing others pass him, 'but now,' as he wrote to Cowell in his later years, 'I am glad to see any man do anything well; and I know that it is my vocation to stand and wait, and know within myself whether it is done well.' Does it ever strike people in these days, when everybody wants to write, that the reader plays an important part too, and that there is nothing ignoble in accepting it? Good books cannot do their work without good readers, and many people might be good readers who are now indifferent writers. Anyhow, FitzGerald was not above accepting that part, and if it led in his case to writing, and writing well, that was almost an accident and one to which he himself attached no importance. The part for which he cast himself was that of spectator. And his instinct was a sound one. His leisureliness is the root of what is finest in his writing and most lovable in his life. He is the wise and kindly looker-on in an age when hardly any one gives himself time to look about him, any more than a set of jockeys riding a race. The rest of us who are in the stream cannot see it; he was on the bank, and could. And that was what gave him the ripe gift of meditation, the note of a man who had thought long and often on deep questions, that is the distinction of such poems as *Omar* and the *Bird Parliament*.

Why, by the way, has this last poem never enjoyed, not the whole, but its fair share, of the popularity of *Omar*? It contains so many things of the sort that are most remembered in the *Rubaiyat*, moral or mystical epilogues, some-

times crying the same call of vanity of vanities, and
sometimes, again, piercing right through the spiritual veil
in the way of the great mystics, saying things not to be
forgotten by the ear, not so easily remembered or realized
by the character and will. Is it that Attar is without
Omar's poignant pessimism? Or is it that the heroic
couplet cannot produce the moving effect of that astonishing stanza? Something of both, no doubt. The *Bird Parliament* has certainly neither the imaginative power of the
Rubaiyat nor its haunting felicity of phrase. But it has
things which ought to have made it better known than it
is. It is for ever striking the note of the mystics, as in
the lines which read like a reply to some self-righteous
Calvinist, sure and certain of his heavenly 'election':—

> But he was sternly checkt. 'I tell thee this:
> Such Boast is no Assurance of such Bliss:
> Thou canst not even fill the sail of Prayer
> Unless from *Him* breathe that authentic Air
> That shall lift up the Curtain that divides
> His Lover from the Harim where *He* hides—
> And the Fulfilment of thy Vows must be,
> Not from thy Love for Him, but His for Thee.'

Or take the last lines of the apologue of the Moths, who
send messengers to find their Idol, the Flame, and the first
and second come back with slight and uncertain intelligence
and are rejected, and a third goes in their place

> who, spurr'd with true Desire,
> Plunging at once into the sacred Fire,
> Folded his Wings within, till he became
> One Colour and one Substance with the Flame.
> He only knew the Flame who in it burn'd;
> And only He could tell who ne'er to tell return'd.

Or, once more, there is the better-known passage in which
human life is compared to a child carrying a torch on a dark
and windy night;

> For like a Child sent with a fluttering Light
> To feel his way along a gusty Night
> Man walks the World: again and yet again
> The Lamp shall be by Fits of Passion slain:
> But shall not He who sent him from the Door
> Relight the Lamp once more, and yet once more?

No man would, or could, have written these things, whether his own or Attar's, without that meditative gift which belongs only to people who have plenty of time to think, and belonged so conspicuously to FitzGerald. When the flippant inquirer asked the old monk what he had been doing all his life, he replied, *Cogitavi dies antiquos et annos aeternos in mente habui.* That was a flight above Fitz-Gerald. But that he had his kinship with it is shown by his liking for these mystical Persians. Attar is, of course, more edifying than Omar. Is that part of the reason why he has been so much less popular? They are sometimes very close to each other. The tale of the moths is a very near neighbour to the stanza of *Omar*:—

> Strange, is it not? that of the myriads who
> Before us pass'd the door of Darkness through,
>   Not one returns to tell us of the Road,
> Which to discover we must travel too.

And there are other parallels. But, whatever the resemblances, and whatever the merits of the *Bird Parliament*, it must be admitted that it contains few or none of these Shakespearean passages in which *Omar* abounds. In the *Bird Parliament* we never get quite into the world of 'we are such stuff as dreams are made on' as we indisputably do in

> We are no other than a moving row
> Of Magic Shadow-shapes that come and go
>   Round with the Sun-illumin'd Lantern held
> In Midnight by the Master of the Show.

That is the real distinction, no doubt, that gives *Omar* its supremacy. Here, as in Shakespeare, whenever thought, imagination, and language are joined together in this three-fold cord of perfection there is no resisting them.

But after all what we think of most in this centenary is not the poet but the man. The birth that took place on March 31, 1809, carried with it no promise of a translator of Omar; its promise was that of the life of a human being. How richly that promise was kept! We shall half forget the poet's fame next Wednesday as we recall the loving and lovable nature of the man. Few men's birthdays can be more fitly kept; the gifts that he received at his birth, the innocence and simplicity of childhood, he kept pure and undiminished to the day of his death. Blessed are the pure in heart, the single-hearted, the people who practise no double dealings of thought, or will, or deed. If that be so, it was no mere licensed exaggeration of affection that made George Crabbe, the clergyman, say in announcing the death of the translator of Omar, 'a very noble character has passed away.' But FitzGerald would not have liked us to think of him too gravely. When he had got over his surprise at our thinking of him at all, and perhaps his disgust at our impertinence, he would have begged us, if we must do it, to do it modestly. His only reply to the little fame he got in his life, which came chiefly from America, was to laugh at himself as the 'American Pote'. He liked to describe himself as simply 'a poor devil who is rather too well off'; and would say, as he did once to Pollock, 'I have been all my life apprentice to this heavy business of idleness; and am not yet master of my craft; the gods are too just to suffer that I should.' That was how he saw himself, but no man ever yet saw the whole of anything in the looking-glass. Even as it is it is a pleasant picture, very wholesome for an over-strenuous age. There was happiness enough for FitzGerald in a cottage and a garden without any help from motor-cars or flying machines. His life was securely rooted in old, simple habits. A man of strong affections, he lavished them almost as warmly on the imaginary but ever present friends of his solitude as on the real friends whom he so seldom saw.

No man ever loved good books better. If the spirits of the old poets love to be remembered, FitzGerald's room must often have been charged of an evening with invisible gratitude. 'My dear Virgil', 'my dear Sophocles', 'one loves Virgil somehow'—one may hope that the most august of spirits retain humanity enough to be pleased at such affection. Greater men or greater bibliolaters than he, such men as Gibbon or Macaulay, never strike quite this note. FitzGerald's feeling for Cervantes ('I love the very dictionary in which I had to look out the words'), or for Madame de Sévigné ('my dear old Sévigné'), is, like his feeling for Suffolk and the sea, an affair of the heart. These are the people he spent his life with, an idleness in the best company, talking six languages; the sort of idleness most of us may take off our hats to. If the first and best reason for liking his letters is himself, the second is the company he keeps. To people who care for these things there is a never-ending pleasure, either of agreement or of disagreement, in going through the off-hand originalities which he deals out so impartially, so free-and-easily, as he ranges over his wide country, comparing Greeks and Persians, Spaniards and English, Aeschylus and Sophocles, Reynolds and Gainsborough, Handel and Beethoven, Richardson and Fielding, Shakespeare and Dickens, Scott and Le Sage and Cervantes, Cowper and Walpole, Catullus and Keats. That was his company indoors—and indeed not merely indoors, for when he went to sea he would take Cervantes and Boccaccio, and especially the Greeks, with him. And there is the third reason for liking his letters, that there is so much land and sea in them. The man's affection overflows here too, as it does for his friends and his books. The trees and the streams, the sun and wind and waves, above all the spring, draw words from him that come straight from the heart. The 'trees which all magnanimous Men love'; the sea, which 'likes to be called Θάλασσα better than the wretched word "*Sea*", I am sure'; the radishes at a London breakfast, with which 'comes a savour of earth that brings all the delicious gardens of the world back into one's soul, and almost draws tears from one's eyes'; the landscape he saw from his windows at Geldestone, one, as he tells Cowell, 'which your eyes would drink. It is said there has not been such a Flush of Verdure for years; and they are making hay on the Lawn before the house, so as one wakes to the tune of the Mower's scythe-whetting, and with the old Perfume blowing in at open windows'; they all tell the same tale, the tale of affection and poetry. And they well may, for that is, in fact, in this field as in all the rest, the tale of FitzGerald's life.

MEREDITH'S POETRY [1]

PERHAPS the best sort of congratulation a great man can receive on his birthday is an assurance that his work lives and that men and women live by it. At any rate, in the case of Mr. Meredith, one would be inclined to feel sure that that sort must be the most acceptable. He is one of the two living veterans of English literature whom we all rejoice in honouring; and the truest honour we can pay him is to do our best to know and use his work. Most people would take that to mean his novels, and so it does. But it means other things too. Indeed, there could hardly be a stronger proof of the extravagant ascendency which the novel still possesses over all other literary forms than the fact that Mr. Meredith is thought of almost exclusively as our greatest novelist. Every one knows his novels, but only the few who go to seek literature wherever they can find it have much acquaintance with his poetry. Yet poetry has, on the whole, proved so much the most lasting of the forms of creative human speech that it may well be that *Love in the Valley* may be remembered at least as long as *The Egoist*. *Rasselas* had in its day many more readers than *The Vanity of Human Wishes*; and Sidney was long thought of as the author of the *Arcadia*, and not as the writer of the Sonnets to Stella; but in each case, for us to-day, the verse has a stronger life than the prose. The fact, perhaps, is that the pleasurable excitement afforded by metre, and the higher mood in which poetry is usually written, carry us into an atmosphere in which we are less conscious of changed fashions in thought and expression than we inevitably are

[1] Feb. 13, 1908.

in prose. There is in poetry an element of strangeness
which makes us ready to welcome a certain unlikeness to
our ways of speech and our own point of view. But that
is not so in prose. The fancies which are delightful in
Elizabethan verse are only tolerable in the contemporary
prose; the conceits which we endure in Donne or Cowley
would not be endured in any writer who was not a poet.
Perhaps the truth is that, with contemporaries, prose has
a better chance than verse, other things being equal; with
posterity, other things being equal, verse has a better chance
than prose. But when all explanations have been given, it
remains a strange thing that Mr. Meredith is still, even after
Mr. George Trevelyan's ardent and interesting exposition of
his poetic gospel, so little known to the outer circle of readers
of poetry. Perhaps no poet of his calibre has ever continued
writing verse so long with so little public recognition. That
is the first fact about him which seems to ask for some
explanation. Why are his poems so little known?

There is no need, we are afraid, to go very far in the
search for an answer. Three-fourths of his poetry is, to say
the least, extremely difficult to understand. Even more
often than Browning, he writes as if the art of poetry con-
sisted in throwing down before the reader a jumble of words
to be disentangled at leisure. In particular, he is needlessly
perverse in the order of his sentences, abusing the licence of
transposing subject and object, which is so dangerous in
English where no change of termination distinguishes
nominative from accusative. The result is an intolerable
obscurity, as in the lines—

> Wherefore their soul in me, or mine,
> Through self-forgetfulness divine,
> In them, that song aloft maintains.

But this is only one special form of a fault which everywhere
stands in his way. How many of his readers can make anything of such things as—

> A woman who is wife despotic lords
> Count faggot at the question, Shall she live?

or,

> Doubt you with the monster's fry
> All his orbit may exclude.

How long do people of fair intelligence take to discover the meaning of *The Song of Theodolinda*, even with the poet's note to help them? And this obscurity is unhappily not confined to a few poems. Indeed, there is hardly anything except the delightful *Juggling Jerry* which does not contain some extremely difficult lines. It is impossible not to feel that Mr. Meredith might have played a far greater part as a poet in the life of the nation if he had but cared to add intelligibility to his other great qualities. Has he ever soothed himself with the deceitful consolation that great utterances are necessarily obscure? Never was a greater delusion. The object of poetry is the highest kind of pleasure; the noblest passages of Dante, Shakespeare, and Milton are nearly always the simplest; the very easiest of the Odes of Pindar is one of the grandest of all. The message of the poets is to all the world; let them never forget to leave crabbed utterances to those whose message is only to the schools.

Yet Mr. Meredith is a true and great poet. There is no living man who can be thought of as his rival in power of mind, in virile energy of conviction, in originality of insight into this wild-seeming, sound-hearted Earth on whose soil we live. But this very strength brings its limitations. He is too strong to help the weak. He has a Pagan disregard of those who fail, who are in moral or intellectual difficulties, who are unhappy. And so such people, always a large part of our poor humanity, will turn away from his exultant and irritating force to Arnold for sympathy, to Wordsworth for healing. The gift he brings is one of stimulus alone. Then, again, his atmosphere is always highly and subtly intellectualized; he knows little of the large primal simplicities of the human heart, by which Wordsworth makes so immediate and universal an appeal. In a kind of lyrical energy he more resembles Shelley, but the resolutely physical basis of his thought will always separate him from the most spiritual, almost unearthly, of poets. Yet, rare as the love of soul is, it is not so rare as the love of mind, and it is not only because he is a greater poet that Shelley will always have a larger audience than Mr. Meredith.

In what direction, then, does his poetic strength lie? Not in heart, but in head: not in sympathy, but in will: not in the power to console, but in the power to compel. It is a gospel of vitality that he proclaims, and he cares for little else. He has little of the special interest in morals which is a nearly unbroken tradition of English poetry; and if he is, as he is always, on the side of the moral laws, it is not so much for their own sake as because the other path is the path of weakness and failure. 'Quit yourselves like men; be strong,' is the text of all his sermons. Some who can feel that to be the greatest of all texts will say that few indeed are the sermons in verse that can rival *The Empty Purse*, *A Faith on Trial*, or the magnificent *France, 1870*. And that is true, true for those that have ears to hear. In the last, above all, he has caught the great accent of the Seers, and we seem to hear again the Hebrew prophet or the Aeschylean chorus, as he cries with a solemn simplicity too seldom his—

> Forgetful is green earth; the Gods alone
> Remember everlastingly; they strike
> Remorselessly and ever like for like.
> By their great memories the Gods are known.

But this is the great morality of the primal universal type, too large and general, too distantly august, to supply the place of the other for which we must not look to Mr. Meredith—the small morality, of whose reproof and strength and

comfort most of us feel such bitter need on the everyday
path of life.

> Not she gives the tear for the tear;
> Harsh wisdom gives Earth, no more;
> In one the spur and the curb;
> An answer to thoughts or deeds;
> To the Legends an alien look:
> To the Questions a figure of clay.
> Yet we have but to see and hear,
> Crave we her medical herb.
> For the road to her soul is the Real:
> The root of the growth of man:
> And the senses must traverse it fresh
> With a love that no scourge shall abate,
> To reach the lone heights where we scan
> In the mind's rarer vision this flesh;
> In the charge of the Mother our fate;
> Her law as the one common weal.

It may all be true, perhaps, and certainly no ignoble truth;
but it is not, in any case, one we can always be brave enough
to listen to; none of us very often, indeed, and some never;
and then we have dreamt of something more human behind
the visible veil, of a Love which is yet to be the ultimate
reading of the hard mysteries of life.   But of mere Earth,
or mere Brain—the only stuff Meredith would employ—no
such figure can be woven.   Thousands who have lived by
Wordsworth's gift of faith, Arnold's of endurance, Tennyson's
of wisdom, Browning's of joy, will turn away from this proffer
of strength as one not receivable by human sorrow till other
gifts have gone before it.   The religions that have conquered
the world are not those which have proclaimed strength, but
those that have consoled weakness.

But if Mr. Meredith's key to the riddle is not one for all
times or for all people, it is no theft or copy, but the natural
product of his own strong will and brain.   Tennyson made
natural science, in which he was so much more than a student,
suggest a solution beyond nature, one which science could

neither discover nor disprove. Mr. Meredith has tried the
harder task of aiming at one strictly confined to natural
bounds. Only time can show whether Humanity can ever
rest in such solutions. But even if they cannot give man
a home, they can at least be the inn which refreshes him on
the homeward journey. And from the upper windows of it
there is even a sight of home in the far beautiful distance ;
where the 'Child of the Death and the Life' may learn

> What issue may come of the two :—
> A morn beyond mornings, beyond all reach
> Of emotional arms at the stretch to enfold :
> A firmament passing our visible blue.
> To those having nought to reflect it, 'tis nought ;
> To those who are misty, 'tis mist on the beach
> From the billow withdrawing ; to those who see
> Earth, our mother, in thought,
> Her spirit it is, our key.

The Earth of his creed and affection is indeed no bare prison-
house of matter, nor even a mere palace of the senses. She
can point her votaries beyond the visible, provided they do
not ask too much for their own individual selves. She is like
the Nature he gives us in *Modern Love*, who goes 'laughing
on her way', and cries—

> I play for Seasons ; not Eternities—

and we are to trust her and love her, even though our lot may
be that of the leaf that falls, learning to rejoice that we have
served the great Whole by moving and shining through the
sunlight of our summer, and to believe that we shall serve It
still by laying ourselves down in the mould. Our only way
either of safety or of duty is to accept the teaching of Earth
not in part but in its entirety. We only have to

> read her thought to speed the race,
> And stars rush forth of blackest night :
> You chill not at a cold embrace
> To come, nor dread a dubious might.

Her double visage, double voice,
In oneness rise to quench the doubt.
This breath, her gift, has only choice
Of service, breathe we in or out.

Since Pain and Pleasure on each hand
Led our wild steps from slimy rock
To yonder sweeps of gardenland,
We breathe but to be sword or block.

The sighting brain her good decree
Accepts; obeys those guides, in faith,
By reason hourly fed, that she,
To some the clod, to some the wraith,

Is more, no mask; a flame, a stream.
Flame, stream, are we, in mid career
From torrent source, delirious dream,
To heaven-reflecting currents clear.

And why the sons of Strength have been
Her cherished offspring ever; how
The Spirit served by her is seen
Through Law; perusing love will show.

Love born of knowledge, love that gains
Vitality as Earth it mates,
The meaning of the Pleasures, Pains,
The Life, the Death, illuminates.

For love we Earth, then serve we all;
Her mystic secret then is ours;
We fall, or view our treasures fall,
Unclouded, as beholds her flowers

Earth, from a night of frosty wreck,
Enrobed in morning's mounted fire,
When lowly, with a broken neck,
The crocus lays her cheek to mire.

But for this last stanza the passages we have so far quoted
might give the impression that he cared only for the strength
and sternness of Earth, and thought little of her beauty. But
that is a long way from the truth. He does, perhaps, teach
and preach and argue about her a little too much, but no one

can make the surrender to the spell of her beauty more completely than he. That may be known indeed through the
novels to those who have never read a line of his verse. And,
fiercely as he likes to declare his adhesion to the bare facts
of her, he will take her beautiful things and give them back
to us drenched with a dew of human emotion that might
come from Keats himself. Who that has ever read of it has
forgotten the stream that ran through Beckley Park, whose
'view was sweet and pleasant to Evan Harrington as wind-
ing in and out, to east, to north, it wound to embowered
hopes in the lover's mind, to tender dreams'. Of the 'Golden
lie the meadows: golden run the streams' of Richard Feverel
there is no need to ask the question, nor of much else. It is
true that there is nothing in the poems quite so perfect as
these enchanted islands of the novels; and it is strange, as
some of his admirers think, that his greatest handling of the
human drama should be no novel, but a set of sonnets, and
his nearest approaches to that beauty which is the visible
form of the harmony of Heaven and Earth and the Human
Soul should not be poems at all, but prose passages in the
novels. Still the poet of *Love in the Valley*, *The Lark Ascend-
ing*, *The Woods of Westermain*, *The Day of the Daughter of
Hades*, *Phoebus with Admetus*, *Melampus*, *The South-Wester*,
The Thrush in February, is a great poet, not only, in his own
phrase, of the 'Joy of the Earth', but also of her beauty. It
is true that he never attains to the divine spontaneity with
which the greatest men have handled Nature. Here, as
everywhere in him, the intellect overweights not only the
imagination but even the soul, so that he cannot attain
to that melodious union of all the forces which supreme
poetry demands. He seems too often to be giving us the
fresh observation, the original thought, which had the
making of a great poem or great passage in them; but it is
not made. It is with him as with his own Orson of the
Muse (was he thinking of Whitman?):—

Him when he blows of Earth, and Man, and Fate,
The Muse will hearken to with graver ear
Than many of her train can waken : him
Would fain have taught what fruitful things and dear
Must sink beneath the tidewaves, of their weight,
If in no vessel built for sea they swim.

So that his poetry does not lend itself easily to quotation. Its
greatness is commonly in the fine stuff of which it is made,
and in a continuous stream of rushing energy, not in anything which will stay to be looked at. Yet now and then he
will give us work of the kind that invites the pause and
the picture. Could there be more wonderful proof of the
immortal freshness of the great themes of poetry than that
Mr. Meredith and Mr. Bridges in this late day have touched
once more the lark and the nightingale, and found inspiration in them for their best and freshest work? Mr. Meredith
is assuredly never more a poet and never more himself than
when he interprets for us the song of the lark :—

For singing till his heaven fills,
'Tis love of earth that he instils,
And ever winging up and up,
Our valley is his golden cup,
And he the wine which overflows
To lift us with him as he goes:
The woods and brooks, the sheep and kine,
He is, the hills, the human line,
The meadows green, the fallows brown,
The dreams of labour in the town;
He sings the sap, the quickened veins;
The wedding song of sun and rains
He is, the dance of children, thanks
Of sowers, shout of primrose-banks,
And eye of violets while they breathe;
All these the circling song will wreathe,
And you shall hear the herb and tree,
The better heart of men shall see,
Shall feel celestially, as long
As you crave nothing save the song.

Who has uttered better than this one of the best of Nature's

voices, one in which man will always think he catches some
sympathy with his own ?   Poetry more than anything else
takes us back and down to that inner part of man which is
unchanging under all external change; and though it may
seem a long way from the ancient poet thinking of his
message as before all things heavenly and divine to this
modern seer thinking of his as essentially human and of
earth, yet are we really here so very far in spirit from the
little hills that long ago rejoiced on every side and the
valleys that stood so thick with corn that they must laugh
and sing ?

This, then, is Mr. Meredith the poet ; a great preacher of
a strong, stern creed ; a profound student of human life and
the human drama ; a voice as of a fountain bubbling up out
of the heart of earth herself, not always clear, but always
keen and fresh.   Everywhere his genius is more lyrical than
dramatic, for he is himself always the first of the *dramatis
personae*; but he now and then gives proof of the dramatist's
power of vividly realizing a great situation, as in the magnificent *Nuptials of Attila*.   And he is one other thing also.
His magnificent political odes have recalled the great days
of Shelley's *Liberty*, Wordsworth's Sonnets, and Coleridge's
France.   They unite the youth's ardour and intense hold on
the present with the seer's vision brooding over time and
eternity.   There has been nothing like them in the last
hundred years.   Tennyson was indeed the ideal voice of
English political wisdom, but these issues did not greatly
move him ; and Mr. Kipling has kept in the main to an
altogether lower level.   But these glorious French odes seem
to bear us up away from the dusky lights of earth, which are
all the politician has to guide himself by, into the very
splendour of the heavens.   They quiver with sympathy,
they burn with righteousness, they even have at times the
stately motion of their own poet's ' army of unalterable law '.
No poet has ever come more triumphantly out of the difficult

field of contemporary politics.   And there is another thing.
The history the poets have given us has generally been
more poetical than historical.   That has not been the case
with Mr. Meredith.   There is no sketch of Napoleon in
existence that contains so much of the essential truth about
him as Mr. Meredith's ode.   Everything that Napoleon was
to France, and France to him, of curse and blessing, is there,
nothing extenuated and nothing set down in malice, however
sternly one-sided the balance ultimately falls.   The only
criticism to make on it is that it is perhaps a little too
tumultuous; we are everywhere in the whirlwind and the
storm; there is too little of the delightful ease of great
poetry; but then it may be that that mighty ghost is not to
be raised without the whirlwind's help.   Magnificent, however, as this ode is, the finest of the four is certainly the
France, December 1870; and we can leave no better
impression of the poet's greatness than by quoting one more
passage from this noble poem:—

Ever invoking fire from heaven, the fire
Has grasped her, unconsumable, but framed
For all the ecstacies of suffering dire.
Mother of Pride, her sanctuary shamed;
Mother of Delicacy, and made a mark
For outrage; Mother of Luxury, stripped stark;
Mother of Heroes, bondsmen; thro' the rains,
Across her boundaries, lo the league-long chains!
Fond Mother of her martial youth; they pass,
Are spectres in her sight, are mown as grass!
Mother of Honour, and dishonoured; Mother
Of Glory, she condemned to crown with bays
Her victor, and be fountain of his praise.
Is there another curse? There is another:
Compassionate her madness: is she not
Mother of Reason? she that sees them mown
Like grass, her young ones! Yea, in the low groan
And under the fixed thunder of this hour
Which holds the animate world in one foul blot
Tranced circumambient while relentless Power
Beaks at her heart and claws her limbs down-thrown,

She, with the plunging lightnings overshot,
With madness for an armour against pain,
With milkless breasts for little ones athirst;
And round her all her noblest dying in vain,
Mother of Reason is she, trebly cursed,
To feel, to see, to justify the blow;
Chamber to chamber of her sequent brain
Gives answer of the cause of her great woe,
Inexorably echoing thro' the vaults,
'Tis thus they reap in blood, in blood who sow;
This is the sum of self-absolvèd faults.'
Doubt not that thro' her grief, with sight supreme,
Thro' her delirium and despair's last dream,
Thro' pride, thro' bright illusion, and the brood
Bewildering of her various Motherhood,
The high, strong light within her, tho' she bleeds,
Traces the letters of returned misdeeds.
She sees what seed long sown, ripened of late,
Bears this fierce crop; and she discerns her fate
From origin to agony, and on
As far as the wave washes long and wan
Off one disastrous impulse; for of waves
Our life is, and our deeds are pregnant graves
Blown rolling to the sunset from the dawn.